More LITTLE TALKS ABOUT GOD & YOU

V. GILBERT BEERS

ILLUSTRATED BY JAN CIELOHA

HARVEST HOUSE PUBLISHERS
Eugene, Oregon 97402

Scripture quotations are taken from the Holy Bible, New International Version, Copyright © 1978 by the New York International Bible Society. Used by permission of Zondervan Bible Publishers.

MORE LITTLE TALKS ABOUT GOD AND YOU

Copyright © 1987 V. Gilbert Beers
Published by Harvest House Publishers
Eugene, Oregon 97402

Library of Congress Catalog Card Number 87-081042
ISBN 0-89081-586-0

Printed in the United States of America.

FOR PARENTS AND TEACHERS

The nest is empty. Last fall Cindy left for college, ending a 32-year stretch of having children in the house. It was time now to reflect on parenting. What would we do, and not do, if we were starting again?

I was still reflecting on this when Cindy came home for the weekend. She and Arlie and I instinctively settled down for one of our little talks. This was not a planned, formal conversation, but a spontaneous kind of talk that we had enjoyed with our children through the years. There had been hundreds, perhaps thousands, of these little talks—sprawled on the floor, walking through the woods, riding in the car, hiking, canoeing, swimming, biking, sledding, or whatever.

"You know, not many of the kids at school talk like this with their parents," Cindy volunteered. We agreed that what we had was warm and wonderful and had begun many years before. This kind of thing begins as soon as children learn to talk. To put it another way, if you want to have delightful, rewarding talks with your children when they are older, you must begin to have them when your children are younger.

So many of our little talks through the years have focused on God and the many wonderful things He has done for us. That makes it easy for God, His Word, and His ways to become a natural part of everyday conversation, and a mini-course in theology unfolds for the growing child.

This book and its companion are little talks which you will enjoy with your growing child. They embrace much theology and Bible doctrine, but in a conversational mode for a young child.

The greatest heritage that you and I can give to our children is the freedom to talk about God and His Word and His ways, with the delight that is often not associated with spiritual matters.

Start now, with one of these little talks each day. You will begin a lifelong relationship with your child that will become increasingly rewarding. Your child will also begin a lifelong relationship with the Lord that will become eternally rewarding.

—V. Gilbert Beers

More
LITTLE TALKS
ABOUT
GOD & YOU

Where Is God When I Pray?

"Where is God when I pray?" Elise asked her mother.

"Where do you think He is?" asked Mother.

"Sometimes I think He is near," said Elise. "But sometimes I think He must be so far away that He can't hear me."

What would you tell Elise?

A Little Talk about Where God Is

1. Have you ever wondered how close or how far away God is when you pray?
2. What do you think Mother will say to Elise?

"The Bible tells us that the Lord is near to all who pray to Him," said Mother. "Whenever you pray, He comes near to hear."

"Does that mean He always listens?" asked Elise.

"Yes, that's why He comes near," said Mother. "He wants to listen to everything you say to Him."

"I'm glad He cares so much for me," said Elise. "I'm glad He loves me so much that He listens when I pray."

A Little Talk about God and You

1. When was the last time you talked with God? What did you talk about? Why did you want Him to listen?
2. Do you think God heard what you said? What makes you think that He did?

BIBLE READING: Psalm 145:17-19.

BIBLE TRUTH: The Lord is near to all who call on Him. He hears their prayer and helps them. From Psalm 145:18,19.

PRAYER: Thank You, dear God, for being near me and for hearing my prayer. I'm glad that You love me so much that You listen when I pray. Amen.

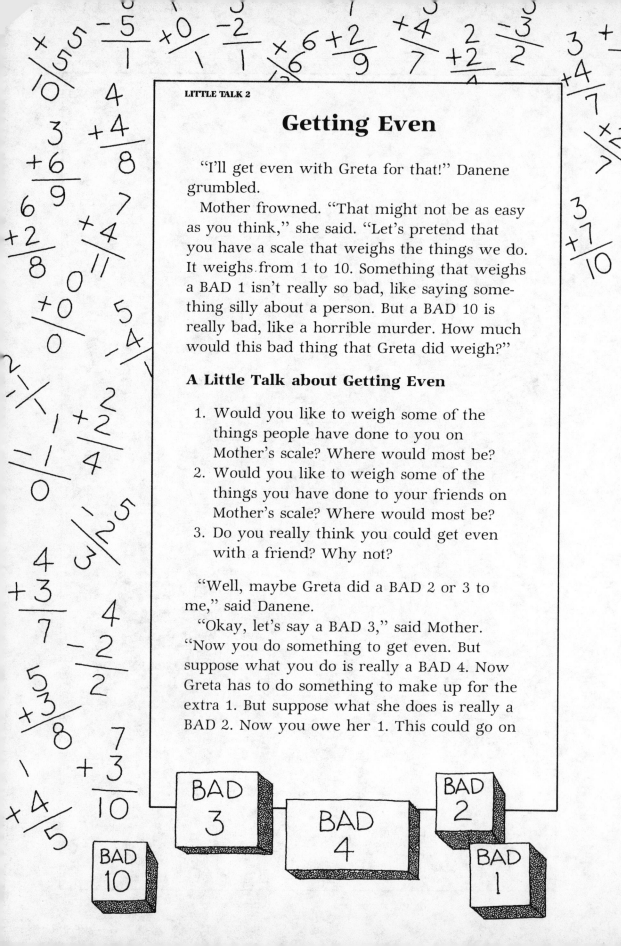

LITTLE TALK 2

Getting Even

"I'll get even with Greta for that!" Danene grumbled.

Mother frowned. "That might not be as easy as you think," she said. "Let's pretend that you have a scale that weighs the things we do. It weighs from 1 to 10. Something that weighs a BAD 1 isn't really so bad, like saying something silly about a person. But a BAD 10 is really bad, like a horrible murder. How much would this bad thing that Greta did weigh?"

A Little Talk about Getting Even

1. Would you like to weigh some of the things people have done to you on Mother's scale? Where would most be?
2. Would you like to weigh some of the things you have done to your friends on Mother's scale? Where would most be?
3. Do you really think you could get even with a friend? Why not?

"Well, maybe Greta did a BAD 2 or 3 to me," said Danene.

"Okay, let's say a BAD 3," said Mother. "Now you do something to get even. But suppose what you do is really a BAD 4. Now Greta has to do something to make up for the extra 1. But suppose what she does is really a BAD 2. Now you owe her 1. This could go on for a long time. Do you think you will ever really get even?"

Danene smiled. "That won't work," she said. "But what should I do?"

"Instead of doing a BAD 3 to get even with her BAD 3, do a GOOD 2 for her," said Mother. "Now she owes you 5 on your scale. Before long, she will do something good to 'get even' on the good things rather than on the bad things."

So Danene began to think of some good things she could do for Greta.

A Little Talk about Jesus and You

1. What are some bad things we do to Jesus? Has Jesus ever done any bad things to us?
2. What are some good things Jesus has done for us? What are some good things we can do for Jesus? Will our good things ever weigh as much as Jesus' good things?
3. Why doesn't Jesus want us to try to "get even" with the bad things that other people do to us?

BIBLE READING: Matthew 5:43-48.

BIBLE TRUTH: Don't try to pay back evil with evil. From Romans 12:17.

PRAYER: Dear Jesus, help me to do good to my friends when they do bad things to me. I know that is what You would do. Amen.

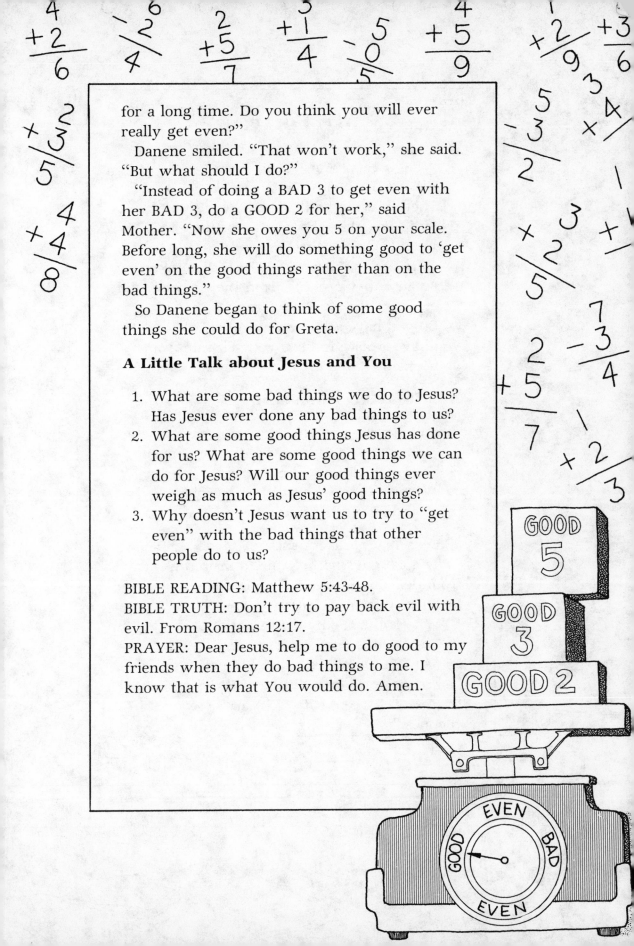

My Fortress

"What a good story!" said Ryan.

"What is it about?" Father asked.

"There is a big battle," said Ryan. "Just when it looks like the good guys have lost, they get back into the fortress."

"Why is that so important?" Father asked.

"Because they are safe from the enemy," said Ryan.

"Do you have a fortress?" Father asked. "Do you have a place to keep yourself safe from your enemies?"

A Little Talk about a Fortress

1. Why was the fortress so important for the "good guys"? What would have happened if they had not had a fortress?
2. What do you think Father meant when he asked Ryan if he had a fortress?

"Everyone needs a fortress," Father said. "The good guys needed one to keep the enemy from defeating them. But you need one to keep the enemy from defeating you, too."

"Who is the enemy?" Ryan asked.

"The devil is our biggest enemy," said Father. "But we have many little enemies, like hatred or greed or selfishness. We need a fortress to keep us safe from all these enemies."

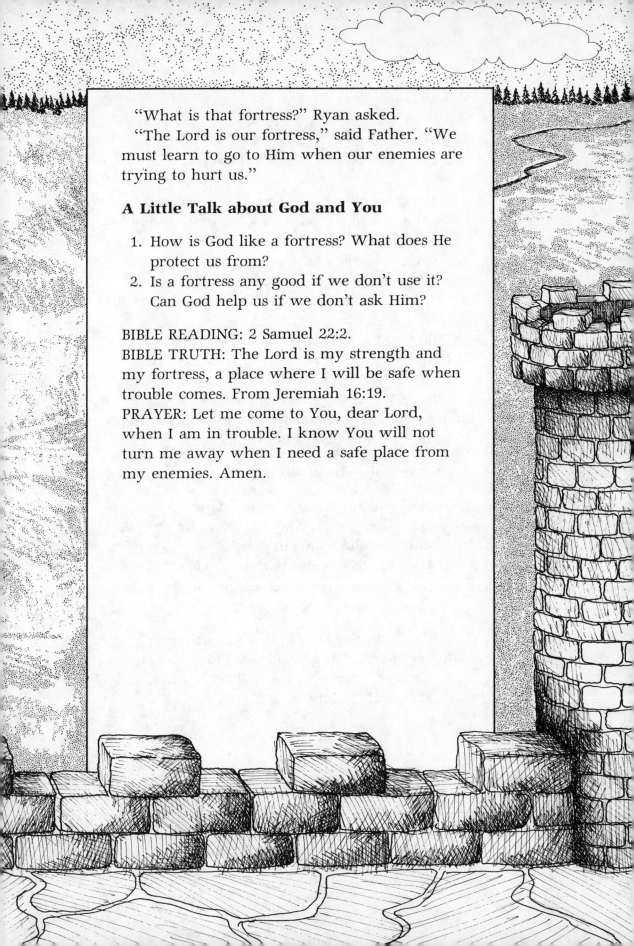

"What is that fortress?" Ryan asked.

"The Lord is our fortress," said Father. "We must learn to go to Him when our enemies are trying to hurt us."

A Little Talk about God and You

1. How is God like a fortress? What does He protect us from?
2. Is a fortress any good if we don't use it? Can God help us if we don't ask Him?

BIBLE READING: 2 Samuel 22:2.

BIBLE TRUTH: The Lord is my strength and my fortress, a place where I will be safe when trouble comes. From Jeremiah 16:19.

PRAYER: Let me come to You, dear Lord, when I am in trouble. I know You will not turn me away when I need a safe place from my enemies. Amen.

How Much Money Should I Give?

"Margaret always puts a dollar in the offering at Sunday school," said Susan. "I put in only a quarter."

"Is that as much as you can give, or as much as you *want* to give?" Mother asked.

"That's as much as I can give," said Susan. "I want to give much more."

"Do you think the dollar is as much as Margaret can give, or as much as she wants to give?" Mother asked.

"Margaret has lots and lots of money," said Susan. "She doesn't want to give the dollar, but her mother makes her do it."

A Little Talk about Giving

1. How much money does Margaret give? Does she give all she can? Does she give as much as she wants to give?
2. How much money does Susan give? Does she give all she can? Does she give as much as she wants to give?

"Which do you think pleases Jesus more?" Mother asked. "To give all you can, but want to give more? Or to give less than you can, and not even want to give that?"

Susan smiled. "I guess it's better to give all you can, and want to give more," she said. "I guess that's what I'm doing now."

A Little Talk about Jesus and You

1. Which girl was pleasing Jesus more? Why?
2. Would Jesus rather have less money that you want to give, or more money that you don't want to give?
3. Do you love to give to Jesus? If you do, that pleases Him very much, no matter how much you can give.

BIBLE READING: 2 Corinthians 9:6-8.
BIBLE TRUTH: Give what you want to give, not what you think you should give. God wants only what you really want to give Him. From 2 Corinthians 9:7.
PRAYER: Dear Jesus, thank You for giving me what You wanted to give, not what You thought You had to give. May I be willing to give to You and Your friends the same way. Amen.

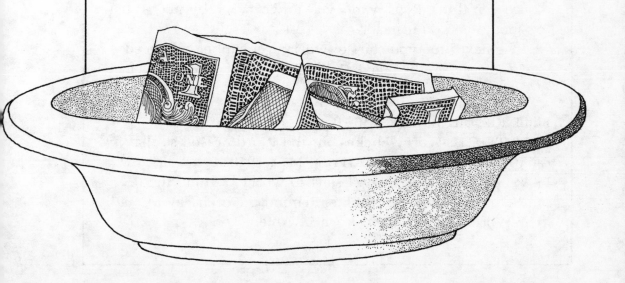

Weeds and Flowers

Debra and Grandma were picking wild-flowers one day. Suddenly they came to a big patch of weeds.

"The next time you worry, remember these weeds," Grandma told Debra.

Debra looked puzzled. "Why?" she asked.

A Little Talk about Worry

1. Do you ever worry? What about?
2. Would you rather worry or would you rather stop worrying?
3. What do you think Debra's grandma meant when she said, "The next time you worry, remember these weeds"?

"Worry is like weeds," said Grandma. "It chokes out the beautiful things in our lives. It even chokes out God's Word."

Debra looked at the weed patch. She could not see any beautiful wildflowers growing there. There was nothing but weeds.

"Yuk," said Debra. "I don't want a lot of weeds in my life. I want God's Word to grow in my life instead."

A Little Talk about Jesus and You

1. Do you think Jesus wants you to worry? Why not? What should you do instead?
2. The next time you start to worry, remember the weeds. Would you rather have God's Word or worry weeds in your life? Why?

BIBLE READING: Mark 4:13-20.
BIBLE TRUTH: Worry chokes out the Word of God so that it can't bear fruit in our lives. From Mark 4:18,19.
PRAYER: Dear Jesus, when I start to worry, remind me to put Your Word first in my life. Remind me each day to read Your Word, the Bible, and learn it. Amen.

Helpers

Rod wanted to go with the rest of the family. Trips with the family were so much fun.

"But I can't," Rod said. "I promised Mr. Hoskins that I would feed his horses and give them water. That will take two hours. By the time I finish, it will be too late for me to go."

This was a problem. Rod's family was going to a place more than a hundred miles away.

Do you have any ideas about helping Rod to go on his family trip? Should Rod tell Mr. Hoskins he fed the horses but not do it?

A Little Talk about Helping

1. Why shouldn't Rod say that he fed the horses if he didn't? What would you like to tell him?
2. Can you think of any way that Rod can go on his family's trip? Is there some way the family could be helpers?

"I have an idea," said Rod's brother. "Let's all go over and help Rod feed the horses. There are four of us, so we could get it done in about 30 minutes. Then we can all go on the trip together."

Do you think this is a good idea? Rod's family thought it was. So that is what they did. They all fed the horses together and they all went on their trip together.

A Little Talk about God and You

1. What do you like about the way Rod's family did this? Why would you like your family to do this if you were Rod?
2. Why do you think God was pleased with the way Rod's family did this?

BIBLE READING: Isaiah 41:6.
BIBLE TRUTH: Each helps the other, and says to his brother, "Be strong." From Isaiah 41:6.
PRAYER: Dear God, I want other people to help me when I need it, so remind me to help others when they need it. Amen.

Strong Soap

Sandy touched something greasy in the garage. When she came into the house, she left big greasy fingerprints on the white kitchen door.

"I'll clean it," Sandy told Mother.

Sandy took some paper towels and put water on them. She rubbed and she scrubbed, but the water did not take the greasy fingerprints off the white door.

Mother smiled. "You need something stronger to wash those fingerprints away."

"Okay, I'll use soap," Sandy said. She did not think to ask Mother what to use.

Sandy rubbed the wet paper towels on some soap. Then she rubbed and scrubbed the kitchen door. But the greasy fingerprints would not come off.

What would you like to tell Sandy?

A Little Talk about Washing

1. Why didn't water take the greasy fingerprints from the door? Why didn't soap take them off?
2. What do you think Sandy should use? Why?

"Do you have something that will take those greasy fingerprints off the door?" Sandy asked Mother.

Mother smiled. "I thought you would never ask," she said. Then Mother gave Sandy a plastic bottle.

"Spray some of this on," she said. "Then wipe it off with paper towels." When Sandy did that, the greasy fingerprints went away.

"Wow, that's strong soap!" said Sandy. "Is this the strongest soap there is?"

"No, there is a soap that will wash your sins away," she said. "It is much stronger than this. You might call it Jesus soap. He is the only One who can wash our sins away."

"I'm glad He has done that for me," said Sandy. Are you?

A Little Talk about Jesus and You

1. Have you ever asked Jesus to wash your sins away? Don't try to do that yourself. It's like washing greasy fingerprints with water.
2. Would you like to ask Jesus to do this now?

BIBLE READING: 1 John 1:7.
BIBLE TRUTH: Jesus is the only One who has power to wash our sins from us. From Matthew 9:6.
PRAYER: Dear Jesus, thank You for washing my sins away. I want to tell others You can do that for them too. Amen.

Grandma's Knitting

"Grandma, you knit the most beautiful things on earth!" said Kelly.

Grandma smiled. "You're sweet, Kelly," she said. "I have won some nice ribbons at the fairs, and I do like to knit. But there are many things that are more beautiful than my knitting."

"What?" Kelly asked.

A Little Talk about Beautiful Things

1. Does your mother or grandmother make beautiful fancywork? Do they knit, or crochet, or paint, or do other beautiful things like those?
2. Can you think of designs that are even more beautiful than knitting and other fancywork?

"Come with me," Grandma said to Kelly. Grandma took a magnifying glass with her.

When they went into the yard, Grandma stopped at the big maple tree. Then she pulled a leaf from one of its branches.

"Let's look at this fancywork," said Grandma. Kelly looked at the leaf with the magnifying glass.

"Oh, it's so beautiful!" she said. "Look at all those wonderful designs!"

Next Grandma found a rose. Kelly was so excited when she looked at the rose through the magnifying glass. Grandma and Kelly looked at many beautiful things, such as bark on the oak tree, a blade of grass, and even the puffy white dandelion ball.

"Now you see why I said there are more beautiful things than my fancywork," said Grandma. "And you know who made them all."

"God does make the most beautiful things of all," said Kelly.

A Little Talk about God and You

1. Have you ever looked at a leaf or a rose or a blade of grass through a magnifying glass? Would you like to do that? What do you see that you don't see without the magnifying glass?
2. Who made these beautiful things? Have you thanked Him for them? Would you like to do that now?

BIBLE READING: Genesis 1:29-31.
BIBLE TRUTH: God saw all the beautiful things He had made, and they were very good. From Genesis 1:31.
PRAYER: Thank You, dear God, for making a rose, and a blade of grass, and all the beautiful things that I can see each day. Each time I look at one of these beautiful things, I will remember You. Amen.

What Happened to the Balloons?

Leo watched his little sister play with her red balloon. The more he watched, the more he wanted it.

Leo already had a green balloon, but he wanted a red one. So before his sister knew what was happening, he grabbed her red balloon and took it away from her.

But Leo's sister grabbed back.

BANG went the red balloon. BANG went the green balloon. Now Leo had no balloons. And Leo's sister had no balloons.

"That is called covetousness," Father said. Leo looked up. Father was standing in the doorway. He had seen the whole thing.

Do you know what covetousness is?

A Little Talk about Coveting

1. Coveting is wanting what someone else has. Have you ever done that? What did you want that someone else had?
2. Why is it wrong to covet? Does it hurt someone else? Does it hurt you when you covet?

"The Bible says we must not covet," said Father. "If we take something that does not belong to us, we hurt the other person, just like you hurt your sister by breaking her balloon."

"I'm sorry," said Leo. "I really did not want to hurt her."

"Of course not," said Father. "People usually do not want to hurt others, but it happens. And they often hurt themselves, too, just as you lost your own balloon."

That was true. Now Leo and his sister were hurt because of his covetousness. Each had a balloon before, but now neither had a balloon.

What would you like to say to Leo?

A Little Talk about Jesus and You

1. Do you think Jesus coveted anything? Why not?
2. Do you think Jesus is pleased when we covet something? Why not?

BIBLE READING: Luke 12:15.
BIBLE TRUTH: You must not covet. From Exodus 20:17.
PRAYER: Help me, dear Jesus, not to want what other people have. I know this will hurt me and the other person, and You will not be pleased. Amen.

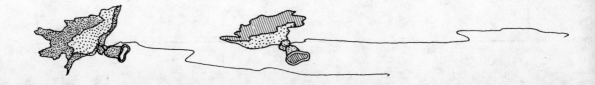

Someone Like God?

"That man must be as good as God," said Beth.

Mother looked surprised. "Do you know how good God is?" she asked.

Beth thought awhile. She really did not know how good God is.

"Is anyone as good as God?" Beth asked Mother.

A Little Talk about Being Good

1. Who is the best person you have ever known? Do you think that person is as good as God? Why not?
2. Can anyone be as good as God? Why not?

"Every person does something wrong," said Mother. "Each time we do something wrong, we know that we are not as good as God."

"So I really can't say someone is as good as God, can I?" said Beth.

"Not unless you know someone who has never done anything wrong," said Mother.

Beth thought for a long time. But she could not think of anyone who had never done anything wrong. Beth even had a long list of things that she herself had done wrong. So she could not think of anyone who was as good as God.

A Little Talk about God and You

1. How good is God? Has He ever done anything wrong?
2. How good are you? Have you ever done anything wrong? Do you know anyone but God who has never done anything wrong?

BIBLE READING: Isaiah 40:21-25.
BIBLE TRUTH: We can't compare anyone with God. No one is equal to Him. From Isaiah 40:25.
PRAYER: Dear God, I'm glad You love me. Thank You! Amen.

Love Is Patient

Nate was showing his little sister how to make a tower with some blocks. But each time she tried to do it, the tower fell over.

Nate became angry and knocked over all the blocks and stomped out of the room. But he almost bumped into Father in the doorway.

"Trouble?" asked Father.

"She can't learn," Nate grumbled.

"Really?" said Father. "Usually she is quite bright. Could it be that she is not learning what you want as fast as you want?"

A Little Talk about Patience

1. What did Nate say about his little sister? What did Father say about her? Who do you think is right?
2. Do you ever lose patience with your brother or sister? Why? What should you do instead?

Nate thought about what Father had said. It was true that he had lost his patience because his sister had not learned what he wanted. And she had not learned as fast as he wanted. Nate thought that his little sister should learn as fast as he did.

"Love is patient," said Father. "That's what we learn in 1 Corinthians 13:4."

"Are you saying I don't love my little sister?" Nate asked.

"No," said Father. "This Bible verse is not saying that. It is saying that you should be patient with people you do love. You love your little sister, so you should be patient with her."

A Little Talk about God and You

1. Think of three people you love. Why would you not like to lose your patience and get angry at any of them?
2. Why would you not want God to lose His patience and get angry at you? Why do you want Him to be patient with you? If you want God to be patient with you, shouldn't you be patient with other people?

BIBLE READING: 1 Corinthians 13:4.
BIBLE TRUTH: Love is patient. From 1 Corinthians 13:4.
PRAYER: Dear God, help me to be as patient with others as I want You to be with me. Amen.

The Strongest Man

"I want to be the strongest man in the world!" said Jody.

"That's easy," said Jody's father.

Jody looked surprised. "It is?" he asked. "I thought it would be hard to do. Don't I have to do exercises and stuff?"

"That will give you a strong body," said Father. "But you said you wanted to be a strong man. Which do you want?"

A Little Talk about Being Strong

1. What does Jody want to become? Do you think he really wants to have a strong body, or instead be a strong person? What is the difference?
2. Would you rather have a strong body or instead become a strong person?

"I guess I really want to be a strong person," said Jody. "But how do you do that?"

"The Bible tells us," said Father. "The Lord helps us become strong. And being happy with Him makes us especially strong. That's called the joy of the Lord."

"Then that's what I want," said Jody. "I want to be happy with the Lord. I want the joy of the Lord if that will make me strong."

A Little Talk about God and You

1. What if you are always angry at the Lord, or unhappy with Him? Will that help you become a strong person?
2. What if you are not pleasing the Lord? What if you know that you are not doing the things that will make the Lord happy? Will that help you become a strong person?
3. Would you like to become a strong person? Then love the Lord and do things that please Him.

BIBLE READING: Psalm 27:1.
BIBLE TRUTH: The joy of the Lord is your strength. From Nehemiah 8:10.
PRAYER: Dear Lord, help me to please You with my life. As I do, teach me to know Your joy. Then I will be strong. Amen.

Did God Make Any Ugly Places?

"What an ugly place!" said Louise. "Why did God make such an ugly place?"

"He didn't," said Father. "God doesn't make ugly places. We do."

A Little Talk about God's Creation

1. What is the most ugly place you have ever seen? What made it ugly?
2. What is the most beautiful place you have ever seen? What made it beautiful?

"Look closely at this place and tell me what makes it ugly," Father said to Louise.

Louise looked at all the things that made the place ugly. There were cans and paper lying under a tree. An old tire lay across a fence. The fence was broken in places. Louise saw many other things that made the place look ugly. Every one of them was there because people had done something wrong.

"I guess God didn't do any of the ugly things here," said Louise.

"Now look closely at this place and tell me what you see here that is beautiful," said Father.

Louise looked around. There was a clump of

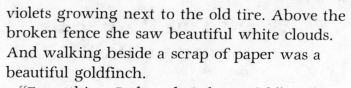

violets growing next to the old tire. Above the broken fence she saw beautiful white clouds. And walking beside a scrap of paper was a beautiful goldfinch.

"Everything God made is beautiful," said Louise. Don't you think that is true?

A Little Talk about God and You

1. Do you think God made anything ugly in His world? Can you think of any ugly thing that God made? If you look closely, even creatures such as toads and salamanders have a special beauty.
2. When you see an ugly place, ask who made it ugly, people or God. Do you help to keep God's world beautiful? Do you try to keep it from getting ugly?

BIBLE READING: Ecclesiastes 3:11.
BIBLE TRUTH: God has made everything beautiful. From Ecclesiastes 3:11.
PRAYER: Thank You, dear God, for the beauty of Your creation. Help me to keep it that way. Amen.

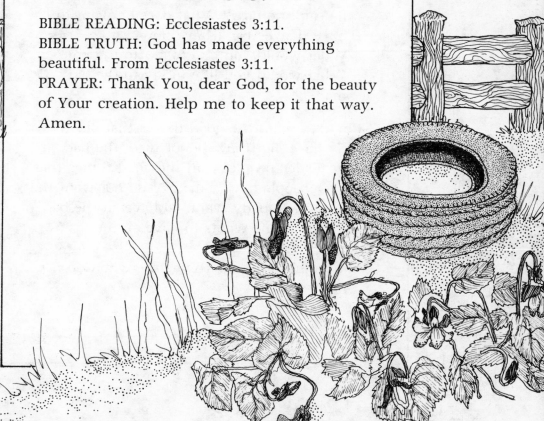

Would You Rather Be Young or Old?

"I wish I was older," a boy said.

"I wish I was younger," an old man said.

Who do you think is right, the boy who wants to be older or the old man who wants to be younger?

A Little Talk about How Old We Are

1. Why do you think the boy wants to be older? What does he want to do that he can't do now? What does he want to have that he can't have now?
2. Why do you think the old man wants to be younger? What does he want to do that he can't do now? What does he want to have that he can't have now?
3. What would you like to say to the boy? What would you like to say to the old man?

Children want the good things that older people have. But they do not want the bad things. Older people want the good things that younger people have. But they do not want the bad things. Nobody wants to have all the bad things. Everyone wants to have all the good things.

But we have to take things the way God

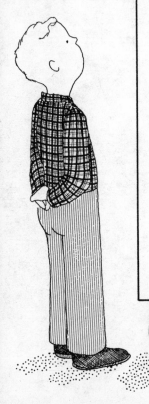

made them, don't we? Boys and girls can do
some good things that older people can't do.
And older people can do some good things that
boys and girls can't do.

Let's be happy the way we are! That's the
way God made us.

A Little Talk about God and You

1. The Bible tells us that younger people are
   strong. They can run and jump and play.
   Old people can't do that as well.
2. But old people with white hair are wiser.
   They often know what is best. They can
   help people decide what to do when they
   need help. Younger people can't do that
   as well. They haven't seen as many things.
   They have not lived with the Lord as many
   years.

BIBLE READING: Proverbs 20:29.
BIBLE TRUTH: The crown of a young man is
strength. The crown of an old person is white
hair. From Proverbs 20:29.
PRAYER: Dear Lord, help me to be happy with
my age. And help me to keep on being happy
as my age changes each year. Amen.

Are You Listening?

"You need a sweater for your school trip today," Mother told Christopher. "The weather forecast said it will become very cool this afternoon."

"None of the other guys will wear a sweater on a warm spring day like this," Christopher argued. "They will all think I'm a sissy or something."

Christopher would not listen to Mother. No matter what she said, Christopher would not wear his sweater.

Has this ever happened to you?

A Little Talk about Listening to Advice

1. Has Mother or Father ever said you should do something, but you did not want to do it? What happened?
2. Why should you listen to Mother or Father? Why do they know some things that you don't?

That afternoon Christopher ran into the house. He was sneezing and blowing his nose.

"Is something the matter?" Mother asked.

"It was so cold on that trip!" Christopher said. "I think I caught cold. I should have listened to you. Everyone else had a sweater."

Do you think Christopher learned something important?

A Little Talk about God and You

1. Where does God give us some important advice? Do you read your Bible so that you know what God wants to tell you?
2. Why is it important to listen to God's good advice? Will you?

BIBLE READING: Proverbs 12:15.

BIBLE TRUTH: A wise person listens to advice. From Proverbs 12:15.

PRAYER: Dear God, give me the good sense to listen to my parents and You. Thank You for loving me enough to tell me what to do. Amen.

When Will God Answer?

"God will listen to your prayers and will answer them," Mother said.

"That's not true," said Carol. "I prayed for something and God did not answer me."

Mother looked surprised. "Really?" she asked. "When did you pray?"

"Last night!" said Carol.

A Little Talk about Answered Prayer

1. What do you think about the way God is answering Carol's prayer?
2. Have you prayed for something that you thought God did not give to you? What was it? Did you expect Him to answer right away or did you wait patiently for Him to answer in His own good timing?

"If God answers your prayer tomorrow, is He still answering it?" Mother asked.

"Yes," said Carol. "I suppose He is."

"If God answers your prayer next week, is He still answering it?" Mother asked.

"Yes," said Carol.

"If God answers your prayer next year, is He still answering it?" Mother asked.

Carol smiled. "Are you saying I am expecting His answer too soon?" said Carol.

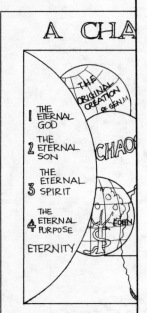

A CHA... ...TIME

THE ORIGINAL CREATION OF GEN. 1:1

CHAOS

EDEN

1 THE ETERNAL GOD

2 THE ETERNAL SON

3 THE ETERNAL SPIRIT

4 THE ETERNAL PURPOSE

ETERNITY

"God may be answering today," said Mother. "He may be saying no. But He may not answer for some time. We must learn to wait patiently."

A Little Talk about God and You

1. What did Mother say about the way God answers prayer? Does He always give us what we want? Why not? Does He always answer today or tomorrow? Why not?
2. What does it mean to wait patiently for the Lord? Will you?

BIBLE READING: Psalm 37:5-7.
BIBLE TRUTH: Be still before the Lord and wait patiently for Him. From Psalm 37:7.
PRAYER: Dear God, thank You for listening to my prayers. Help me to wait patiently for Your answer, even if Your answer is no. Amen.

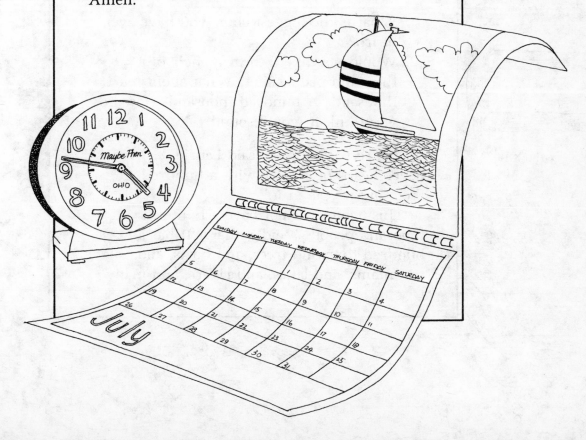

The Whole Earth Is a Choir

"There must have been a hundred people in our church choir this morning!" said Laurie. "It was so wonderful!"

Father smiled. "As a matter of fact, I counted them," he said. "There were exactly 40 people. But it was beautiful."

"I wonder what it would sound like if there were a hundred people in the choir," said Laurie.

"What if there were a hundred thousand in the choir?" asked Father.

Laurie laughed. "There couldn't be a choir that big," she said.

"Yes, there is a much bigger choir that sings every day," replied Father.

A Little Talk about Singing

1. What is the biggest choir you have ever heard?
2. Would you like to hear a choir of a thousand people sing? What about ten thousand? A hundred thousand? How do you think it would sound?

"You're teasing me," said Laurie. "I have never heard of a choir with a hundred thousand people in it."

"This choir does not have a hundred thousand people," said Father. "It has a hundred thousand trees, and birds, and mountains, and lakes, and rivers, and many

other things. The Bible tells us that the whole earth is a great choir that sings to God. We can't hear it all, but He can."

"Oh, I wish I could hear the whole earth sing to God!" said Laurie. "It must be wonderful!"

"We can hear little parts," said Father. "We hear the birds singing, the sound of the rushing stream, the soft sighing of the wind, and many of God's creatures joining in. But God hears the whole choir."

Then Father and Mother and Laurie sang these words from their hymnal: "This is my Father's world, and to my listening ears, all nature sings, and round me rings the music of the spheres."

A Little Talk about God and You

1. Listen to the sounds around you. How many things can you hear singing to God and you?
2. Scientists tell us that there are many sounds that we don't hear, even out in space. God hears many wonderful songs that we do not hear. Would you like to hear the whole world singing to Him?

BIBLE READING: Psalm 96:11-13.
BIBLE TRUTH: Sing to the Lord, all the earth. From Psalm 96:1.
PRAYER: Dear Lord, I want to sing too. Let me sing with the whole earth as it sings praises to You. Amen.

Looking through God's Eyes

Gwen had to choose one other girl to play on her team. She looked at one girl who was clean and neat, but her clothes were very ordinary. It was clear that this girl came from a poor family that could not afford to buy nice clothes.

Gwen looked at another girl who had beautiful clothes. Anyone could see that this girl's mother bought her clothes in the very best stores.

Each girl was a good team person. Which girl do you think Gwen chose?

A Little Talk about Rich and Poor

1. Do you have both rich friends and poor friends? Does it matter to you if your friends have very nice clothing or just ordinary clothing? Do more of your friends have very nice clothing, or do more of them have ordinary clothing?
2. Would you like to say something to Gwen before she chooses a girl for her team? What would you like to tell her?

Gwen almost chose the girl with the very nice clothing. She liked this girl very much. And she would do well on the team.

People 👁 👁 outside

But then Gwen looked at the other girl. She wasn't chosen very often. Many of her friends didn't seem to notice this girl because of her ordinary clothes. When Gwen wondered what Jesus would do, she chose the girl with the ordinary clothes. She knew the leader on the other team would probably be glad to choose the girl with the nice clothes. Do you think Gwen did the right thing?

A Little Talk about Jesus and You

1. Do you think Jesus would choose someone because of clothing? Do you think He would choose someone because of the kind of person she is?
2. Do you want to be more like Jesus? Should you choose a person because of what he or she wears? Or should you think about the kind of person that he or she is?

BIBLE READING: 1 Samuel 16:7.
BIBLE TRUTH: People look at the outward appearance of others, but the Lord looks at the heart. From 1 Samuel 16:7.
PRAYER: Dear Jesus, when I choose someone to be a friend, help me to look at that person through Your eyes. Let me see that person as You do. Amen.

God 👁 👁 inside

Why Do We Do
What We Do?

Jay's neighbors on one side had a nice car, a beautiful house, and many beautiful things in their house. But they were always bragging about what they had. They bragged about how much money they spent on their things. They bragged about how much more they had than other people. And they bragged about how well they had done in their work.

Jay's neighbors on the other side had a nice car, a beautiful house, and many beautiful things in their house. They had as much as the other neighbors, and their things were just as beautiful. But these neighbors had coffee times in their home to tell people about Jesus. They took their family to church in their car. And they often said, "Thank You, dear God, for these beautiful things. Help us to use them for You."

A Little Talk about the Things We Have

1. Which neighbor pleased God more? Why?
2. Is it all right to have beautiful things? What should we do with the beautiful things God gives us?

"God gives us many beautiful things," Jay's father told him. "He gives us clouds and sunsets and trees. He gives us birds and flowers and green grass. God loves to give His people beautiful things. He also helps us get other beautiful things, like a nice car and a beautiful home."

"But we should remember to thank Him for these beautiful things, shouldn't we?" Jay asked.

"Yes," said Father. "And we need to ask God to help us use our beautiful things to honor Him."

A Little Talk about God and You

1. Who gave you all that you have? Have you thanked God today for all the good things He has given you? Would you like to do that now?
2. How can you use the things that God has given you to honor Him? Can you think of several ways?

BIBLE READING: Deuteronomy 8:17,18.
BIBLE TRUTH: Remember God. He is the One who helps you get money and things. From Deuteronomy 8:18.
PRAYER: Dear God, thank You for helping me and my family get a beautiful home and car and other things. Teach me to use them the way You want me to. Amen.

Which Season Is Best?

"I like spring best," said one boy. "Spring is a time when everything is new. Spring is the time for flowers, robins coming back, and trees in bloom."

"I like summer best," said a second boy. "Summer is the time to go swimming in the pond. Summer is time away from school, and family trips, and walking barefoot in the grass."

"I like fall best," said a third boy. "Fall is the time for pumpkins and apples. Fall is the time to burn leaves and watch the wild geese fly south."

"I like winter best," said a fourth boy. "Winter is the time to go sledding. It is the time to skate on the pond and sit by a fire in the fireplace and drink hot chocolate."

Which season do you like best? Why?

A Little Talk about Seasons

1. Think of three things you like to do each season. Why do you like to do each of these?
2. Did you decide which season is your favorite? Why? What do you like to do most in that season?

"I like something even more special about each season," a fifth boy said.

The first four boys looked surprised. "What?" they asked.

"God made each one," said the fifth boy.

A Little Talk about God and You

1. Why did God make the four seasons? Why not just one?
2. Would you like to thank God for the special things He sends with each season?

BIBLE READING: Genesis 1:14.
BIBLE TRUTH: God made everything beautiful in its season. From Ecclesiastes 3:11.
PRAYER: Dear God, You make so many beautiful things each season. Thank You. Amen.

BIRRAN'S
POND

Will You Rob God?

"That's a mean-looking robber," Mike said when he saw a picture of a robber. The man had a black mask and a gun. Mike was sure he did not want to be near that man!

"What would you think of a robber who came and stole things from our house?" asked Father.

Mike looked angry. "He would be a mean man," he said. "I wouldn't like him."

"What would you think of a robber who stole something from God?" Father asked.

Mike looked surprised. "No one would do that, would he?" he asked.

A Little Talk about Robbing God

1. Have you ever seen a picture of a robber? What did you think of him?
2. What would you think of a robber who took things from your house?
3. What would you think of a person who tried to rob God? What do you think Father meant when he said that?

"The Bible says that many of us rob God," said Father. "You and I may have robbed Him."

Mike looked even more surprised to hear Father say that. "How?" he asked.

"By not giving God the money that belongs to Him," said Father. "Part of what we get belongs to God. If we don't give it to Him, we are robbing Him. That's what the Bible tells us."

Mike was sure that he would never want to rob God. He would be more careful to give God what he should.

A Little Talk about God and You

1. Could you have anything without God's help? All that you have has come because of Him, hasn't it?
2. God wants you to give Him part of what you get. That is called a tithe, or offering. You may give that at Sunday school or church. Or you may give it to someone who uses it for God's work.

BIBLE READING: Malachi 3:8-12.
BIBLE TRUTH: Will a man rob God? From Malachi 3:8.
PRAYER: Dear God, I don't want to rob You. Remind me not to keep what belongs to You. And thank You for giving me all that I have. Amen.

Where Can I Find God?

"I have a new friend," Roy told his father. "This was his first day at school. I want to ask him to come over to play, but I don't know where he lives and I don't know his phone number."

"Does he live near here?" Father asked.

"Yes, but I don't know which house," said Roy. "I looked in the phone book, but his family is not in there yet. I wish I knew where to find him."

A Little Talk about Finding Someone

1. Have you ever wished you could find someone, but couldn't? How do you think Roy feels?
2. Have you ever wished you could find your parents in a crowd, but couldn't? How did that feel?

"Tomorrow be sure to ask your friend for his address and phone number," said Father. "Now you know how it feels to want to find someone and can't. Suppose you wanted to find God and didn't know where to go."

Roy thought about this. Mother and Father had always read the Bible to him. They had taken him to church and Sunday school. But what if they had never done these things? What if he wanted to be friends with God, but didn't know where to find Him?

"I'm going to be sure to tell my friends to read the Bible," said Roy. "And I'm going to invite some of them to come to Sunday school. I don't want them to look for God and not know where to find Him."

A Little Talk about God and You

1. The Bible tells us how to find God. You have heard how to find Him at church and Sunday school. But what if you had never read the Bible, or no one had ever told Bible stories to you? What if you had never gone to church and Sunday school? Where would you look for God then?

2. Would you like to tell some of your friends about Jesus? Would you like to ask them to your church or Sunday school? Would you like to ask if they would read their Bibles?

BIBLE READING: Job 23:3.
BIBLE TRUTH: If only I knew where to find God. If only I knew how to get to His house. From Job 23:3.
PRAYER: Dear God, thank You for sending Jesus to help me go to Your house. Thank You for giving me the Bible, which tells me how to find You and know You. Amen.

LITTLE TALK 23

It's No Fun to Fuss

Mac and Megan were fussing again. They argued about who should be first. Then they argued about who was first last time.

When they didn't have anything to argue about, they argued about that.

What do you think the Bible would say about that?

A Little Talk about Arguing

1. Have you ever argued about something? Was it really important? So why did you argue about it?
2. Have you ever known anyone like Mac and Megan? What would you like to tell them?

"I'm going to make something special for you," Father said one day.

Mac and Megan went to the garage with Father to watch. Father cut a board and sanded it. Then he printed some words on it and painted the words. Then Father put some varnish on the board. He would not let Mac and Megan see what the words said until he was finished.

"May we see it now?" asked Mac.

"Please," said Megan.

PEACE
RYONE ROMANS 12:18

"Come with me," said Father. He took the board into the house and hung it over the doorway between Mac's room and Megan's room. Then he stepped back so Mac and Megan could read it.

This is what the sign says: "Live at peace with everyone." Romans 12:18.

"Does the Bible really say that?" asked Megan.

"Do we have to look at that every time we go into our rooms?" asked Mac.

"Yes and yes," said Father. "Perhaps that will keep you from fussing so much." Do you know what? It did!

A Little Talk about Jesus and You

1. Do you think Jesus argued or fussed with His disciples or His family? Why not?
2. Why is Jesus not pleased when you argue or fuss with your family? What would He rather have you do?

BIBLE READING: Romans 12:18.
BIBLE TRUTH: As much as you can, live at peace with everyone. From Romans 12:18.
PRAYER: Dear Jesus, forgive me when I argue or fuss. Teach me to love my family so much that I will not want to argue or fuss with them. Amen.

What Makes God Angry?

Eric was angry when his little sister got into his puzzles and spilled all the pieces together. You would get angry at something like this too, wouldn't you?

That night Eric began to think. "Does God ever get angry?" he asked Father.

Do you think God ever gets angry? Why?

A Little Talk about Anger

1. What makes you get angry? Do you get angry over things that are not important? Are you ever angry when you shouldn't be?
2. What makes God angry?

"Yes, God does get angry," said Father. "The Bible tells us that He does."

"But what makes God angry?" Eric asked. "Does He get angry when I do little things like my sister did, or only when I do big things?"

"It's not how big or how little," said Father. "God gets angry at evil things, no matter how big or how little. Evil is another way of saying sin, and Jesus died to take sin away. God doesn't want His people to keep sin when Jesus died to take it all away from them."

"I don't want God to be angry," said Eric. "I will try not to keep sin when I have asked Jesus to take it away." That's a good idea, don't you think?

A Little Talk about God and You

1. What makes God angry? Is He angry because a sin is little or big, or because it is a sin?
2. What can we do to keep God from getting angry? What are some things we can do to please God?

BIBLE READING: Romans 1:18-20.
BIBLE TRUTH: God is angry at sin and wickedness because that hides His truth. From Romans 1:18.
PRAYER: Dear God, help me each day to stay away from things that will hide Your truth and make You angry. I really do want to please You. Amen.

Do the Stars Have Names?

As Alan sat beside the campfire with Father, he watched the stars appear one by one.

"God made the stars, didn't He?" Alan asked.

Father smiled. "Yes, He made every one of them. He even gave each star a name."

A Little Talk about the Stars

1. Does God know each person's name? Does He know the name of each of our pets?
2. Do you think God is as concerned about each star as He is about each of our pets? Does He care about a star enough to give it a name?

Alan was quiet for a long time. He watched as more and more stars appeared in the night sky.

"Do we know the names of the stars?" Alan asked at last.

"God did not tell us what He named them," replied Father. "But since He named each star, we know that He cares for each one, just as He cares for us."

"Whenever I see the stars, I will remember that God cares for them," said Alan. "And I will remember that He cares for me, too."

A Little Talk about God and You

1. How do you know that God cares for each star?
2. How do you know that God cares for you?
3. What would you like to say to Him right now? Will you?

BIBLE READING: Isaiah 40:25,26.

BIBLE TRUTH: God brings out the stars one by one, and calls them each by name. From Isaiah 40:26.

PRAYER: Thank You, dear God, for each beautiful star in the sky tonight. As I look at the stars, I will remember You and the way You care for me. Amen.

Will Flowers Bloom Forever?

"Oh, no!" Bonnie moaned. "Look at that beautiful bunch of wildflowers I picked for you. It's all withered."

Mrs. Miller, Bonnie's next-door neighbor, put her arm around Bonnie. "Flowers do wither quickly," she said. "But then most things around us go away unless we help them."

A Little Talk about Dying

1. What happens to wood that causes it to become useless? What about iron?
2. Can you think of other things that become useless if not cared for? What happens to them?

"Wood rots," said Bonnie, "and iron rusts." Then Bonnie thought of many different ways that things become useless.

"What can we do to keep these things from happening?" Mrs. Miller asked.

"Painting helps," said Bonnie. "Oil helps to keep some iron from rusting. Putting flowers in water keeps them from withering."

"Will painting keep wood from rotting forever?" Mrs. Miller asked. "Will water keep flowers from withering forever?"

"Nothing will do that," said Bonnie.

"But God and His Word will never rot, or wither, or fade, or go away," said Mrs. Miller. "Aren't you glad that someone is with us forever and that the 'someone' is God?"

A Little Talk about God and You

1. Are you glad that God never dies? Are you glad that God's Word will never rot, or rust, or wither?
2. Can you think of anything else that never rusts, or rots, or withers? Can you think of anything else that will last forever?

BIBLE READING: Isaiah 40:6-8.
BIBLE TRUTH: Grass withers, flowers fade, but God's Word is there forever. From Isaiah 40:8.
PRAYER: Dear God, I'm glad that You never die or grow old. Thank You for giving us Your Word that never goes away. Amen.

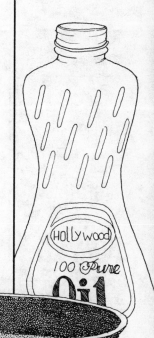

What Do You Hate?

"I hate that bad person," said a boy.

"I hate the bad things that person does," said another boy.

Which boy is right? Which boy is wrong?

A Little Talk about Hating

1. Should we hate any person, even a bad person? Why not?
2. Should we hate bad things that a person does, even though we do not hate the person? Why is this all right?

"God hates sin but loves the sinner," a Sunday school teacher said to the boys. Then the teacher told the boys a story.

Once there was a very bad man who did many bad things. Many people hated him and wished he would die.

One day this very bad man did something so bad that he was put into prison. A man came to the prison and told him that Jesus loved him and even died for him. No one had ever done that before.

So the very bad man accepted Jesus as his Savior. He became a Christian. He stopped doing bad things. He told many people that Jesus loved them. He helped many people become Christians. Now everyone thought he was a very good man. They wished others would be like him.

A Little Talk about God and You

1. Why did people wish the very bad man would die? If he had died at that time, do you think he would have gone to heaven or to hell? Why?

2. What happened to this very bad man? If he died now, at the end of the story, do you think he would go to heaven or hell? Why? Because this man accepted Jesus, will other people go to heaven? Why?

3. Now you see why God loves sinners, but hates sin. Sin will never change. It will always be bad. But sinners can change. They can become God's helpers and bring many other people to know Jesus as Savior.

BIBLE READING: Amos 5:15.
BIBLE TRUTH: Hate evil, but love good. From Amos 5:15.
PRAYER: Dear God, I want to love everyone, as You do. Show me how to tell others to stop doing evil things and turn to You. Amen.

Five Minutes until Sunset

"It's only five minutes until sunset," said Mother.

Jason looked surprised when Mother said that to him. Why was she telling him that?

"You have only five more minutes," Mother said to Jason.

"Five more minutes for what?" he asked.

"Five more minutes to get un-angry at your little sister," said Mother.

A Little Talk about Anger

1. When was the last time you were angry at someone? Why? How long did you stay angry?
2. Why did Mother say that Jason had five minutes to get "un-angry"? What do you think she meant?

"The Bible says you must not let the sun go down on your anger," Mother told Jason. "So you have five more minutes before the sun goes down."

Jason frowned. "Why then?" he asked. "What's so special about sunset?"

"God is telling us that there is a time to stop being angry," said Mother. "What better time than the close of the day? Don't end the day without making sure you have ended it the way God wants you to."

"I guess sunset is as good a time as any to get un-angry," said Jason. Then he went to find his little sister.

A Little Talk about God and You

1. Why does God want us to stop being angry by sunset? Do you know people who just keep on being angry for many days? Why is God not pleased with this?
2. Are you angry at someone? Why? Don't let the sun set today without getting "un-angry" at that person.

BIBLE READING: Ephesians 4:26,27.
BIBLE TRUTH: Don't let the sun go down while you are still angry. From Ephesians 4:26.
PRAYER: Dear God, thank You for setting a time for me to stop being angry. If You didn't, I might keep on being angry for a long time, and that would hurt You and me. Amen.

Are You Ashamed of Someone?

Rick had never thought he was ashamed of Jesus. But one day a friend asked him if he believed in Jesus. Five of Rick's friends were there. Rick knew that not one of them went to church or Sunday school. Not one of them read the Bible. He was sure not one of them believed in Jesus.

Rick looked at his friends. If he said "yes," he was sure his friends would laugh and make fun of him. Without thinking much about it, Rick said "no."

But Rick felt sad all day about this. Do you know why?

A Little Talk about Being Ashamed

1. Why do you think Rick felt sad? What had he done?
2. What would you have said if you were Rick? What would you like to say to Rick now?

At dinner, Rick told Mother and Father what had happened. He told them how sad he felt.

"The Bible tells us why," said Father. "You denied Jesus before your friends. It's like telling a crowd of people that your very special friend is not really your friend at all."

"Do you think Jesus heard what I said?" Rick asked.

"Jesus hears everything we say," Father answered.

"Would Jesus tell His friends that He doesn't know me?" Rick asked.

Then Father read Luke 12:9. Would you like to read this in your Bible?

A Little Talk about Jesus and You

1. Have you ever told someone that you didn't know Jesus, or didn't love Him, or didn't believe in Him?
2. Do you think you would feel sad if you said that? Why?
3. Would you want Jesus to tell His friends that He does not know you, or does not love you? Why not?

BIBLE READING: Luke 12:8,9.

BIBLE TRUTH: Jesus said: "If you tell your friends that you know me and love me, I will tell the angels of heaven that I know you and love you. But if you tell your friends that you do not know me and love me, I will tell the angels of heaven that I do not know you and love you." From Luke 12:8,9.

PRAYER: Dear Jesus, give me the courage to tell my friends how much I love You. Amen.

Yes

How to Talk to an Older Person

Henry did not like the old man across the street. He was sure the man was too old to be any fun. So Henry never walked on that side of the street. That way he never had to talk to the old man.

But one day Henry's ball rolled across the street. It rolled on the old man's lawn. It rolled near the chair where the old man was sitting. The old man picked up Henry's ball.

Henry was sure the old man would yell at him. But he had to get his ball back. So Henry walked up to the old man. He held out his hand.

"Give me back my ball!" Henry shouted at the old man.

A Little Talk about Older People

1. Had the old man done anything unkind to Henry? Did Henry have any good reason not to like the old man?
2. What would you like to say to Henry about this? Do you think Henry is wrong for shouting at the old man? Why?

The old man tossed Henry's ball to him. "I'm sorry to hear you talk like that, " he said softly. "I've watched you many times and I always thought you were a kind young man."

Henry hung his head. He was ashamed of the way he had shouted. "I'm sorry," he told the man.

A Little Talk about Jesus and You

1. Why should we be polite to older people?
2. How would Jesus have talked to the old man?

BIBLE READING: 1 Timothy 5:1.
BIBLE TRUTH: Do not speak harshly to an older man, but speak to him as if he were your father. From 1 Timothy 5:1.
PRAYER: Dear Jesus, help me talk to others as if You were there listening. Amen.

How Long Is Forever?

"How long is forever?" Renee asked.

Father had just read the word "forever" in the Bible. He and Mother and Renee always read the Bible together after dinner.

Do you know how long forever is?

A Little Talk about Forever

1. What would you say if someone asked you how long forever is? Is it a million years? Is it more?
2. Have you ever thought about living in Jesus' home with Him forever? Would you want to be told that you could live there for only a short time? Forever is a long, long time, isn't it?

Father took his long tape measure from the closet and pulled it out a few inches. "Let's say that each inch on this tape measure is 100 years," said Father. "If you live 100 years, you will be very, very old. That's one inch. Now let's pull this out two feet. With 100 years for each inch, that takes us back about 400 years before the time of Jesus."

Renee looked at the two feet. It didn't look like much on Father's long tape measure. Then Father and Renee went out in the yard. Father pulled all the tape out. It was 100 feet long. It almost went across the front of their yard.

"If one inch is 100 years, this long tape is 120,000 years," said Father. "If I had a tape that went all the way across town, then all the way across our state, then all the way across our country, then all the way across the world, eternity would just be starting."

Renee was quiet as she and Father went into the house. At last she said, "Eternity is a long, long time, isn't it? I'm glad I can live all that time with Jesus." Aren't you?

A Little Talk about Jesus and You

1. How many years did Father say his 100-foot tape would be? How many years do you think a tape would be that went around the world?
2. Would you like to live all that time in Jesus' beautiful home in heaven? You can if you have accepted Him as your Savior. If you haven't, would you like to do that now?

BIBLE READING: Psalm 23:6.
BIBLE TRUTH: I will live in the house of the Lord forever. From Psalm 23:6.
PRAYER: Dear Jesus, thank You for being my Savior and Friend. I want to live with You in Your house forever. Amen.

Don't Say That!

Cal was surprised to hear his friend swear. But Cal thought it sounded important. Cal's other friends swore a little also, and Cal wanted to look important to them.

Before Cal knew what had happened, he had said some words that he usually never said. At first Cal thought it made him look important to his friends. But when Cal came home, he began to feel sad about this.

A Little Talk about Bad Words

1. Do any of your friends say words they shouldn't say? Why do you think they do this?
2. Are you ever tempted to say any of these things? Why?

"Why do I feel so sad?" Cal asked his father that night. Then Cal told Father what had happened.

"How do you think Jesus felt when you said those bad words?" Father asked.

"I'm sure He was sad," Cal answered.

"How do you think Mother or I would feel if we had been there and heard you?" Father asked.

"I guess you would have felt sad too," said Cal.

"Perhaps that is why you feel sad," said Father. Do you think Father is right?

A Little Talk about Jesus and You

1. What would Jesus say if He heard Cal swear or say bad words?
2. Do you think Jesus would ever say things like that? Why not? Why shouldn't Jesus' friends say bad words?

BIBLE READING: Matthew 12:35-37.
BIBLE TRUTH: You will have to explain to God why you have said every bad word. From Matthew 12:36.
PRAYER: Dear God, remind me to say words that will please You. Keep me from saying bad words that I will have to explain to You. Amen.

Obey, Even When You Don't Know Why

"Esther, please clean your room this morning," Mother said.

"Why?" asked Esther.

"Because it is important for you to do it," said Mother. Mother could not tell Esther that her grandparents were coming. It was a surprise.

Esther thought that playing was more important than cleaning her room, so she kept on playing. The more she played, the more mess she made in her room.

What would you like to tell Esther now, without telling her the surprise?

A Little Talk about Obeying

1. Why should you obey Mother or Father? Should you obey them only when you know why they are asking you to do something?
2. Why was it important for Esther to clean her room? How do you think she will feel when Grandpa and Grandma see her messy room?

"Surprise!" said Grandpa. Then he and Grandma hurried into Esther's room with their arms out.

Esther ran and hugged Grandpa and Grandma. She was so happy to see them.

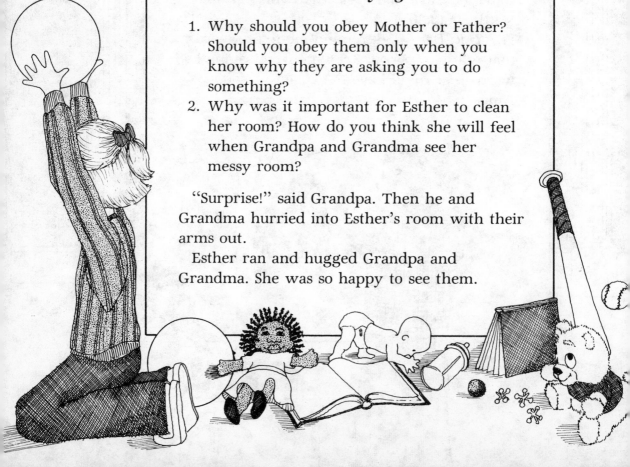

Then Esther looked at her room. It looked terrible. Father had said last night that it looked like the city dump. Now Esther thought Father was right.

Esther wished she had obeyed Mother. She knew now that Mother could not have told her why she should clean her room. That would have spoiled the surprise.

A Little Talk about Jesus and You

1. Why does Jesus want us to obey our parents? Do you think we will learn to obey Jesus if we don't first learn to obey our parents?
2. What do you think Jesus would say to Esther now? Do you think Esther will obey more now?

BIBLE READING: Ephesians 6:1-4.
BIBLE TRUTH: Children, obey your parents in the Lord, for this is right. From Ephesians 6:1.
PRAYER: Dear Jesus, remind me when I disobey my parents or You. I want to obey because I know this will please my parents and You. Amen.

Unfailing Love

Mother bought an electric toaster. But when she plugged it in, it did not work. The toaster failed to do what it was made to do.

Father bought a new camera. But when he pressed the shutter button, nothing happened. The camera would not take pictures. It failed to do what it was made to do.

"So many things don't seem to work," said Michael. "They fail when we need them."

"I'm glad God's love never fails us," said Father. "That's why it is called unfailing love."

A Little Talk about Unfailing Love

1. Have you ever had electric things that didn't work? Have you ever had other things that didn't work? Did they fail you?
2. What did Father mean when he said that God's love never fails us? Does God's love always do what it is supposed to do? Is God's love always there when you need it?

"God's love is unfailing because it is always there when we need it," said Father. "It is unfailing because it always does what it should do for us."

"That should make us feel good," said Michael. "I'm glad something works!"

A Little Talk about God and You

1. When God makes something, it always works the way it should. Have you ever heard of the moon blowing a fuse, or the sun getting a short circuit? Have you ever heard of God's creation needing a repairman to come on a service call to fix it?

2. Does it make you feel good, or comfort you, to know that God's things work the way they should? Does it comfort you to know that His love is unfailing love?

BIBLE READING: Psalm 119:76.
BIBLE TRUTH: Your unfailing love comforts me. From Psalm 119:76.
PRAYER: Dear God, I feel better knowing that Your love, like Your creation, never needs to be fixed. Thank You that Your love never fails. Amen.

Why Todd Was Not Afraid

Ted walked through the woods one night. He was afraid.

Todd walked through the woods one night. But he was not afraid.

Ted was alone when he walked through the woods. But Todd walked through the woods with his father. Why did that make a difference?

A Little Talk about Being Alone

1. Who was with Ted when he walked through the woods? Who was with Todd when he walked through the woods?
2. Why do you think Ted was afraid? Why do you think Todd was not afraid?

Many years ago King David wrote a song. In it he told God, "Even though I walk through the valley of the shadow of death, I will not be afraid, for you are with me" (Psalm 23:4).

Todd was not afraid because he could see his father with him. Ted did not need to be afraid, even though his father was not with him. *God* was with him!

Remember this the next time you are afraid in a strange place. Say to God, "I will not be afraid, for You are with me."

A Little Talk about God and You

1. When is God with you? Is it only part of the time? Or is it all the time?
2. Why shouldn't you be afraid when God is with you? What will you remember the next time you are afraid?

BIBLE READING: Psalm 23:1-4.
BIBLE TRUTH: Even when I walk through places where death seems near, I will not be afraid, for God is with me. From Psalm 23:4.
PRAYER: Dear Lord, You are like a shepherd, protecting me from anything that would hurt me. I will not be afraid because I know You are with me. Amen.

How to Say I Love You

Deena said, "I love you, Mother." Then she did five things that she knew would make Mother unhappy.

Dustin did not say "I love you" to his mother, but he did five things that he knew would make Mother happy.

Which showed more love to Mother, Dustin or Deena?

A Little Talk about Love

1. If we love our parents, should we tell them that we love them? Why is this good?
2. Why was Deena wrong? Was it because of what she said or what she did?
3. Why did Dustin show more love than Deena? Would Dustin's mother like to hear him say "I love you" too?

Deena said "I love you" but did not do things to show that she loved her mother.

Dustin did not say "I love you" but did things to show that he loved his mother.

Would you like to do both? Would you like to say "I love you" and then do things to show that you do? That is the best way, isn't it?

A Little Talk about God and You

1. Did God tell you that He loves you? Where has He said this?
2. Does God do things to show that He loves you?
3. Would you like to tell God that you love Him? Would you like to do some things that show you love Him? Would you like to tell your parents that you love them? Would you like to do some things that show that you love them?

BIBLE READING: John 3:16.
BIBLE TRUTH: Let us not love with words only, but also with the things we do. From 1 John 3:18.
PRAYER: Dear God, You said You loved me, and then You did so many things to show that love to me. When I say "I love You" teach me to do things that show I love You. Amen.

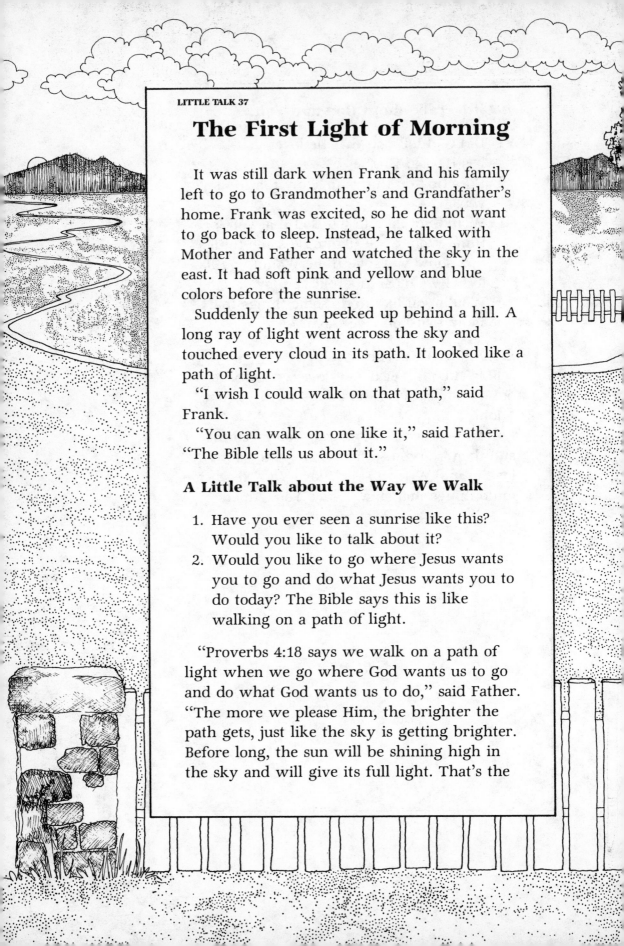

The First Light of Morning

It was still dark when Frank and his family left to go to Grandmother's and Grandfather's home. Frank was excited, so he did not want to go back to sleep. Instead, he talked with Mother and Father and watched the sky in the east. It had soft pink and yellow and blue colors before the sunrise.

Suddenly the sun peeked up behind a hill. A long ray of light went across the sky and touched every cloud in its path. It looked like a path of light.

"I wish I could walk on that path," said Frank.

"You can walk on one like it," said Father. "The Bible tells us about it."

A Little Talk about the Way We Walk

1. Have you ever seen a sunrise like this? Would you like to talk about it?
2. Would you like to go where Jesus wants you to go and do what Jesus wants you to do today? The Bible says this is like walking on a path of light.

"Proverbs 4:18 says we walk on a path of light when we go where God wants us to go and do what God wants us to do," said Father. "The more we please Him, the brighter the path gets, just like the sky is getting brighter. Before long, the sun will be shining high in the sky and will give its full light. That's the way it is when we keep on doing what God wants us to do."

Frank watched the beautiful sunrise. He didn't say anything more for a long time, until the sun was up and the sky was bright.

"I want to do what God wants," said Frank. "I want my life to be like this beautiful sunrise."

A Little Talk about God and You

1. Think of three things that God does not want you to do. Now think of three things that God wants you to do.
2. Which three things are more like the path of light that Frank saw?
3. Why would you rather do the three things that God wants you to do?

BIBLE READING: Proverbs 4:18,19.
BIBLE TRUTH: The path where a Christian walks for God is like the first ray of the sunrise. It keeps on shining brighter until the full light of day. From Proverbs 4:18.
PRAYER: Dear God, shine through me as I do those things that please You so that my life will be like the sunrise. Amen.

God's Chariots

"Look, there's one of God's chariots!" said Father.

Gloria looked up in the sky where Father was pointing. All she could see was a big puffy white cloud.

"I don't see a chariot," said Gloria. "Where is it?"

"There!" said Father. He pointed to the big white cloud.

A Little Talk about God's Creation

1. Do you enjoy watching the clouds? Do you like to watch the wind in the trees? Aren't you glad God made such beautiful things?

2. The whole earth belongs to the Lord, doesn't it? Do you think the Lord delights in the beauty of the earth He has made? Do you think He enjoys His wind, and His clouds, and the other things He has given us?

"Psalm 104:3 tells us that God makes the clouds His chariot and that He rides on the wings of the wind," said Father. "That's

a beautiful way of saying that God is everywhere, even with His clouds and wind."

Gloria looked at the cloud again. "I will
always think that God is near whenever I see a
cloud or hear the wind," she said. Will you?

A Little Talk about God and You

1. How far is God from you? Is He very near?
   Is He near the clouds that you see? Is He
   near the wind you hear?
2. Are you glad that God did not run far
   away from the things He made? Are you
   glad that God did not run far away from
   you when He made you?

BIBLE READING: Psalm 104:1-4.
BIBLE TRUTH: I am with you and will take
care of you wherever you go. From Genesis
28:15.
PRAYER: Thank You, dear God, for staying
with me, and never leaving me alone. Amen.

Don't Try to Bribe Me

"If you play at my house instead of Helen's house, I'll buy you some candy," a friend told Holly.

Holly told Father what her friend said. It didn't sound right, but she asked Father what he thought.

"That is called a bribe," said Father. "It's paying you to do something you don't want to do, or should not do. It doesn't sound like much when someone buys you candy. But in our company a man took some bribes. He lost his job because he did this. He could have gone to prison."

"I don't want to take bribes," said Holly. What do you think Holly will say to her friend?

A Little Talk about Bribes

1. What is a bribe? What did Father say about a man in his company? How was buying candy for Holly a bribe?
2. Why is it wrong to bribe someone? What would you say to Holly's friend who tried to bribe her?

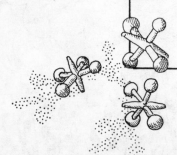

"Thank you for offering me candy," Holly told her friend. "I would like to play with you and Helen. But I will not take candy for playing with a friend. Why don't you and Helen and I play together today?"

Do you think this was a good way to do it?

A Little Talk about God and You

1. Why do you think God would not want you to take a bribe?
2. Did you know that Judas betrayed Jesus for a bribe? Read Mark 14:10,11.

BIBLE READING: Deuteronomy 16:19.
BIBLE TRUTH: Do not accept a bribe, for a bribe blinds you so that you do not see clearly what is right. From Deuteronomy 16:19.
PRAYER: Dear God, help me to see clearly what is right. Then help me do it, not because someone pays me to, but because You want me to. Amen.

Don't Say It if You Don't Mean It!

"Oh, I just *love* your dress!" a woman told Mother.

"I don't think she really likes my dress at all," Mother told Debbie. "She did not seem sincere. She tells everyone the same thing."

A Little Talk about Being Sincere

1. Do you ever tell people that you like something about them? Do you ever tell people that you like something they have? It's nice to say good things about people if you really mean what you say.
2. Do you ever say nice things but don't really mean what you say? Why do you say them?
3. Do you think it is better to say something nice but not mean it, or to say nothing? Why?

"This lady did not need to say anything about my dress," said Mother. "I would rather have her say nothing than say something nice but not mean it."

"I'll remember that," said Debbie. "Nice things are nice only if we really mean what we say."

A Little Talk about God and You

1. What would you think if God says that He loves you, but doesn't really mean it?
2. What would God think if you tell Him that you love Him, but don't really mean it?
3. Why should our love, or saying good things, be sincere?

BIBLE READING: Romans 12:9.

BIBLE TRUTH: Love must be sincere. From Romans 12:9.

PRAYER: Dear God, when You tell me You love me, I know that You mean it. You never say good things unless they are true. Teach me to be like You. Amen.

Who Is Building This House?

"Look, Father, a robin is building her nest in the bush by our house!" said Karla.

Karla and Father watched the robin for a long time.

"How does the robin know what to do?" asked Karla. "Who taught it to build its nest like that?"

A Little Talk about God's Ways

1. Have you watched a robin build a nest? Did it know what to do?
2. Who do you think taught the robin to do this?

"The robin could not build its nest without some very special plans," said Father. "Birds know exactly what to do because God shows them. He is really the architect for every bird's nest. And God shows birds how to get food, too."

Karla kept on watching the robin. "Does God do this only for birds?" she asked.

"No, He does it for every wild animal," said Father. "They all know what to do to make their houses and get food because God shows them how."

"I'm glad God takes care of His birds," said Karla. "Now I know that He will take care of me too."

A Little Talk about God and You

1. How does God take care of the birds and animals?
2. Do you think the birds and animals worry about God taking care of them?
3. Why shouldn't you worry about God taking care of you?

BIBLE READING: Matthew 6:25,26.
BIBLE TRUTH: Look at the birds. They do not plant or store food in barns. But your heavenly Father feeds them. From Matthew 6:26.
PRAYER: Thank You, dear God, for helping the birds build their nests and find food. And thank You for helping take care of me, too. Amen.

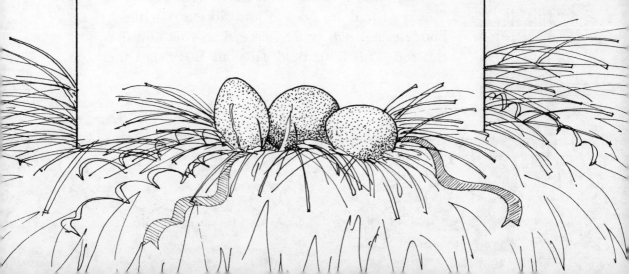

Listen to the Lion Roar!

"Listen to that lion roar!" Paul said to his father. Paul watched the big lion at the zoo. It made a terrible noise as it roared.

"That's a big lion," said Father. "And it has quite a loud roar. But there's another lion that is much more frightening. It has such a terrible roar that it makes this one look like a little pussycat."

Paul's eyes grew big as he listened.

"Where is it?" he asked. "Can I see it?"

A Little Talk about a Roaring Lion

1. What is the biggest lion you have ever seen? Was it at a zoo? Did you hear it roar? Was it loud?
2. Do you know of a much bigger lion somewhere? What do you think Father is talking about?

"This lion is near you right now," said Father. "You cannot see him. You can't even hear him. But he is very fierce. And he wants to hurt you."

"But...but what is this terrible lion?" asked Paul.

"The Bible tells us about him," said Father. "It says the devil goes around like a roaring lion. He is much more fierce than this lion in the zoo. This lion could eat your body. But the devil wants you to turn from God. Then you would not live with God forever. That would hurt you much more than having your body eaten."

"How can I keep him from hurting me?" Paul asked.

"The Bible is the only thing that will protect us from the devil," said Father. "That's because it is God's Word. The devil can't fight that."

Paul was sure that he would read the Bible every day from now on. And he would learn some Bible verses, too. Don't you think that would be good for you to do?

A Little Talk about God and You

1. How is the devil like a roaring lion? What is he trying to do to us?
2. What will protect us from the devil? How can you use God's Word, the Bible, to do that?
3. Would you like to read your Bible each day or have it read to you? Would you like to learn some Bible verses? Will you?

BIBLE READING: 1 Peter 5:8,9.
BIBLE TRUTH: The devil is like a roaring lion.
PRAYER: Dear Jesus, I need Your help. Be with me and help me when the devil comes like a roaring lion to hurt me. Help me to love You and Your Word and to be ready to use Your Word, the Bible, against the devil. Amen.

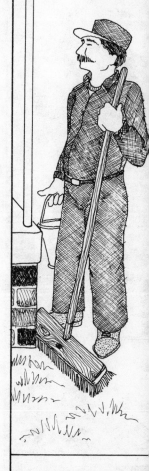

God's Arm around Us

When Billy cut his finger and cried, Mother put her arm around him. She comforted him.

When Tina came home from school crying because her friends made fun of her, Father put his arm around her. He comforted her.

When Mother had a bad headache and cried, Father put his arm around her. He comforted her.

When Father lost his job and felt very sad and lonely, Mother put her arm around him. She comforted him.

Someone else put His arm around each person when that person hurt. Do you know who that is?

A Little Talk about Comfort

1. When was the last time you cried? Why? Did someone put an arm around you to comfort you? Did someone do something else to comfort you?
2. Why are you glad when someone comforts you? Do you think your mother and father and brother and sister like to be comforted too?

The Bible tells us that God "comforts us in all our troubles" (2 Corinthians 1:4). Because He does this, we can comfort other people with the same comfort that God gives us.

God is with us when we hurt. We can't see Him or feel Him, but He has His arm around us, just as Mother or Father puts an arm around us.

Let's remember to comfort others who hurt. We are God's helpers when we do that.

A Little Talk about God and You

1. How do you know that God loves you? How do you know He wants to help you when you are in trouble?
2. When was the last time you were in trouble, or hurt? Did you remember to ask God to help you? Will you remember this the next time you are hurting or in trouble?

BIBLE READING: 2 Corinthians 1:3-5.

BIBLE TRUTH: God comforts us when we have trouble. We can comfort others in trouble the same way that God has comforted us. From 2 Corinthians 1:4.

PRAYER: Dear God, thank You for caring for me when I hurt. I want You near me at all times. But I especially want You near me when I am in trouble. Amen.

How Much Is Enough?

"I wish I had a million dollars," Jim said.

Father smiled. "What would you do with a million dollars?" he asked.

Jim began to make a list. "I would buy a beautiful house for our family," he said. "Then I would buy a couple of new cars." Jim added a few more things to his list.

"Would you be happy if God gave you the million dollars today?" Father asked.

"Oh, yes," said Jim. "I would be the happiest person in the world."

"The Bible says you wouldn't be the happiest person," said Father. "It says you would want more, much more, even if you have a million."

Jim looked surprised. He did not know that this was in the Bible. Did you?

A Little Talk about Wanting More

1. Do you ever wish you had a million dollars? What would you like to do with it?
2. If God gave you a million dollars, would you be satisfied? Or would you want more?

"Here it is," said Father. "Let me read it to you."

Then Father read this from Ecclesiastes 5:10: "Whoever loves money never has money enough; whoever loves wealth is never satisfied with his income."

Jim looked surprised. "Does that mean I can never get enough money?" he asked.

"No," said Father. "You have enough money now. So do I. We have good clothes, good food, a car that runs well, and a warm house, don't we?"

Jim smiled. "I guess we have much more than that. But what does that Bible verse mean, then? Is it wrong to want more?"

"This Bible verse says we should not want more money because we love to have money," said Father. "Sometimes we really need something more, and God wants us to have it. But sometimes we want more just to have more. When that happens, we never get enough."

"Why don't we thank God for what we have now?" said Jim. So they did.

A Little Talk about God and You

1. Is it always wrong to want more? When is it wrong? When is it not wrong?
2. Are you starving? Do you have a warm house or apartment? Do you have clothes to wear? Have you thanked God for these things today? Will you?

BIBLE READING: Ecclesiastes 5:10-12.
BIBLE TRUTH: When you love money, you can never get enough of it. From Ecclesiastes 5:10.
PRAYER: Dear God, thank You for all You have given me. Keep me from loving money because it is money, for I know it will never make me happy. Amen.

Why You Should Not Be Afraid

"But I'm afraid to go to that new school!" Sheila said to her mother.

"All new things make us a little afraid," said Mother. "But when we visited there yesterday, you thought you would like it."

"I will, but I'm still afraid," said Sheila.

A Little Talk about Being Afraid

1. What are some things you have been afraid of this week? Why were you afraid of them?
2. Why is Sheila afraid of her new school? Would you like to say something to Sheila? What would you say?

"Your very best Friend will be there with you," said Mother.

"But I left my best friend when we moved," said Sheila. "She is hundreds of miles away."

"I said your *very* best Friend," said Mother. Then Mother read Isaiah 41:10 to Sheila. Would you like to read this too?

A Little Talk about God and You

1. What does God say in Isaiah 41:10? What does He say about being afraid? Why should you not be afraid when He is with you?
2. Would you like to thank God for being with you as a Friend? Would you like to do that now?

BIBLE READING: Isaiah 41:9-13.
BIBLE TRUTH: Do not be afraid, for I am with you. From Isaiah 41:10.
PRAYER: Dear God, how good it is to know that You are with me in strange places. Thank You that I don't need to be afraid anymore. Amen.

Helping Jesus and One Another

"I need someone to sing next Sunday," said the Sunday school teacher. "Who will do it?"

"Not I," said Darlene. "I'm too busy."

"Not I," said Janie. "I don't want to."

"I'll do my best," said Jan.

Jan sang and did her best. It was good, but it wasn't the best singing the class had heard, and it wasn't the worst.

"I could have done better than that," said Darlene.

"So could I," said Janie.

What would you like to say to Darlene and Janie?

A Little Talk about Doing Our Best

1. Why did Darlene not sing? Why did Janie not sing? Why did Jan sing?
2. What would you say to Darlene and Janie? Why would you say this to them?

A friend heard what Darlene and Janie said. "Why didn't you sing if you could do better?" she asked. "The teacher asked any of us to do it. You should not say unkind things about Jan's singing. She was willing to do it and you were not."

"I'm sorry," said Darlene. "We should not say mean things about friends who do things for Jesus."

"Especially friends who are willing to do things that we did not want to do," said Janie.

A Little Talk about Jesus and You

1. Why does Jesus want us to help do His work? Who will do it if we don't?
2. Do you think Darlene and Janie pleased Jesus when they said unkind things about Jan's singing? Why not? What should Darlene and Janie have done?

BIBLE READING: Galatians 5:13-15.
BIBLE TRUTH: Serve one another in love. If you keep on biting each other, you will hurt each other. From Galatians 5:13,14.
PRAYER: Dear Jesus, I want to help You do Your work. Help me serve my friends, too, and not try to hurt them. Amen.

Would You Fight Yourself?

There was once a king who had a rich, wonderful land. He had a beautiful castle and many good things. This king had about all a king could want.

But the king's son wanted to be the king instead of just a prince. He turned many people against his father. He even tried to kill his father.

Soon half of the people were for the prince, and half were for the king. These people began to fight each other. Many people were killed, and many were hurt. Before long this wonderful kingdom was divided. It would never be the same again.

A Little Talk about Fighting Yourself

1. What caused all the trouble in this kingdom? Did the prince help the kingdom or hurt it?
2. This is a true story, about Absalom rebelling against his father, King David. You may read this story in 2 Samuel 15—18.
3. What would you like to say to this prince? What do you think the prince should have done?

Jesus said that a kingdom or city or family that fights itself will be ruined. Do you know any families that fight? Do you know of any families that have been ruined because of fighting? What should these families have done instead?

A Little Talk about Jesus and You

1. Fighting our own family or city or kingdom or church is like fighting ourselves. Would you fight yourself? Why not?
2. Which of the following would Jesus like us to do: Love one another, pray for one another, help one another, give to one another, say kind things about one another, do kind things for one another?
3. Remember this the next time you think about fighting or quarreling with someone in your family or in your church. Then ask yourself what you should do instead.

BIBLE READING: Matthew 12:25-28.
BIBLE TRUTH: Every kingdom or city or family divided against itself will be ruined. From Matthew 12:25.
PRAYER: Dear Jesus, whenever I want to quarrel with, or fight, my own family, remind me of that ruined kingdom. Then help me to be loving and kind, and to pray instead of fight. Amen.

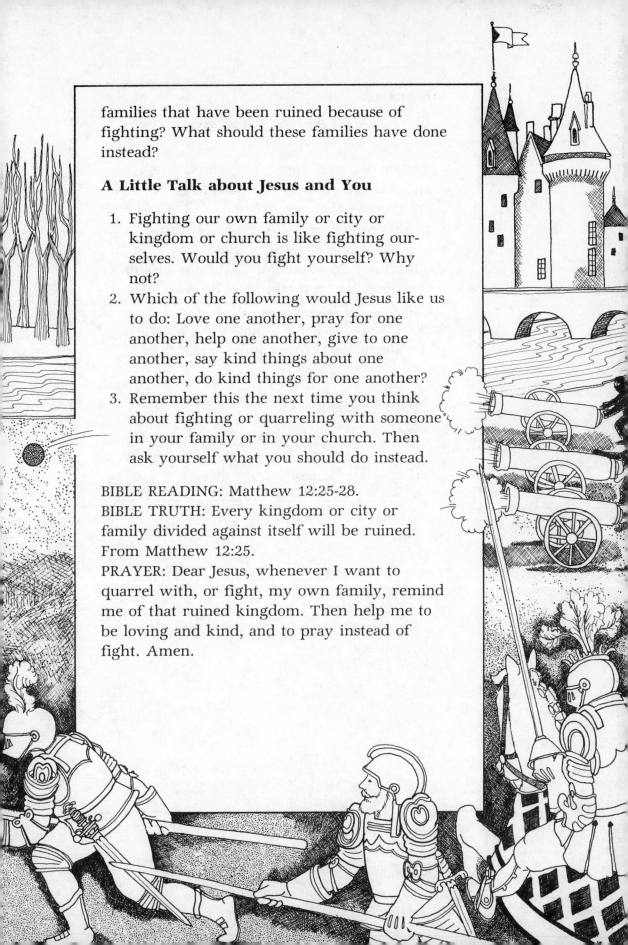

Nothing Undone

Mother was reading about Joshua. "He left nothing undone," she read (Joshua 11:15).

"What does that mean?" Eldon asked.

"Why don't I read all the sentence first," replied Mother. "He left nothing undone of all the Lord told Moses to do. That means he did everything the Lord said must be done."

Eldon was still thinking about "nothing undone" when Mother finished reading.

"Do I ever leave something undone?" he asked.

A Little Talk about Unfinished Work

1. When was the last time you did not finish some work you were supposed to do? Was that work "undone"?
2. What's wrong with "undone" work? Can you think of some "undone" things for Eldon?

"Your shoe was untied when you came to the table this morning," said Mother. "That was undone work. And when you left for school your bed was not made. That was undone work too."

Eldon thought for a moment. "I just remember that I have homework to do tonight," he said. "I don't want to leave that undone."

"And I have to iron some clothes for you for school tomorrow," said Mother. "I don't want to leave that undone either."

So Eldon and Mother hurried away to finish their work. Do you have something you must do now? You don't want to leave it undone, do you?

A Little Talk about Jesus and You

1. What are some things that Jesus wants you to do each day?
2. Are you going to leave any of these undone today?

BIBLE READING: Joshua 11:15.
BIBLE TRUTH: Joshua left nothing undone that the Lord had commanded. From Joshua 11:15.
PRAYER: Dear Jesus, I have thought of several things You want me to do today. Help me not to leave any of these undone. Amen.

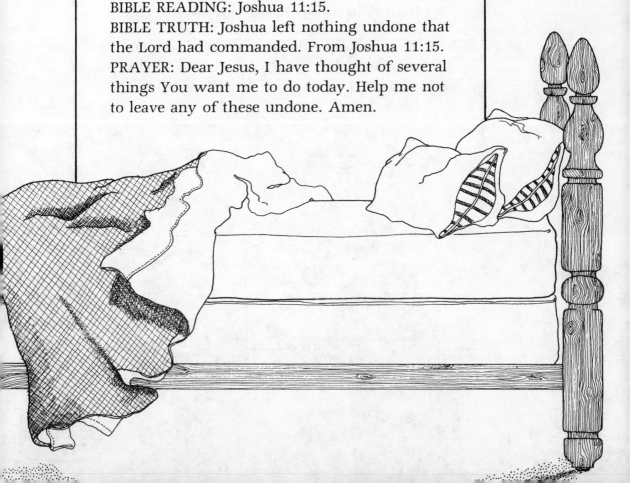

How Long Will God Be Faithful?

"I will be faithful to you as long as I live," a bride told her husband when they got married. And she was! As long as she and her husband lived, she helped him, loved him, worked with him, and did many fun things with him.

"I will be faithful to you as long as I live," a man told his bride when they got married. And he was! As long as he and his wife lived, he helped her, loved her, worked with her, and did many fun things with her.

"I will be faithful to you," God said to His people. How long do you think God will be faithful to us?

A Little Talk about Faithfulness

1. When someone is faithful to us, can we trust him? How long can we trust that person and know that he will not turn against us or hurt us?

2. When a person is faithful, do you have to worry that he will not be with you tomorrow? Do you know that he will be with you as long as you live?

God is faithful to us as long as we live. He will never leave us or turn against us.

But God is more faithful than that. The Bible tells us that He has been faithful to our mothers, grandfathers, great-grandmothers, and great-great-grandfathers. And He will be faithful to your daughters, grandsons, great-granddaughters, and great-great-grandsons. That's a long time to be faithful, isn't it?

A Little Talk about God and You

1. Why do you want God to be faithful to you? When He is faithful to you, what do you expect Him to do? What do you expect Him *not* to do?
2. Why should you be faithful to God? When you are faithful to Him, what should He expect you to do? What should He expect you *not* to do?

BIBLE READING: Psalm 119:90,91.
BIBLE TRUTH: God is faithful through all generations. From Psalm 119:90.
PRAYER: Dear God, I'm so glad I can trust You, as my father and grandmother and great-grandfather trusted You. Thank You for always being there. Amen.

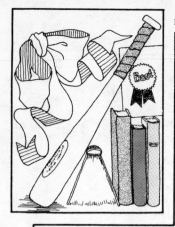

Who Should Say Good Things about You?

"I'm the smartest boy in my class," said a boy.

"I'm the prettiest girl in my school," said a girl.

"I'm the best batter on our team," said another boy.

"I sing better than anyone else in our choir," said another girl.

What would you like to say to each of these boys and girls?

A Little Talk about Saying Good Things

1. Have you ever said, "I'm the smartest, or the prettiest, or the best"?
2. Why shouldn't you say such things? Who should say things like that about you?

The Bible tells us, "Let another praise you, and not your own mouth" (Proverbs 27:2). It doesn't sound good for you to say wonderful things about yourself. That is bragging. But it sounds good for other people to praise us.

There is nothing wrong with that, is there?

A Little Talk about Jesus and You

1. Why does Jesus not want us to brag about ourselves? What is wrong with that?
2. Will you remember this the next time you start to brag? Then say something good about someone else instead. Or say something good about Jesus.

BIBLE READING: Proverbs 27:1,2.

BIBLE TRUTH: Let someone else praise you. Don't do that yourself. From Proverbs 27:2.

PRAYER: Dear Jesus, help me to think of You whenever I want to brag. Remind me that I would have nothing and be nothing if it were not for You. Amen.

Making a Bad Day Good

After Justin tore a hole in his shirt, spilled his milk at the breakfast table, and found a flat tire on his bike, he began to grumble.

"This is a bad day," he complained to Mother.

"No, this is a good day," Mother answered.

"Why do you say that?" Justin asked.

A Little Talk about Bad Days

1. Have you had a bad day? What happened? Why did Justin say this was a bad day? What happened to him?
2. Why do you think Mother said it is a good day? Can you see anything good for Justin?

"There's nothing wrong with the day," said Mother. "You've had several bad things happen to you, but that doesn't make a bad day."

"Well, what's good about it?" Justin asked.

"That's for you to tell me tonight," said Mother. "Will you make a list of all the good things God does for you today and tell me at dinnertime?"

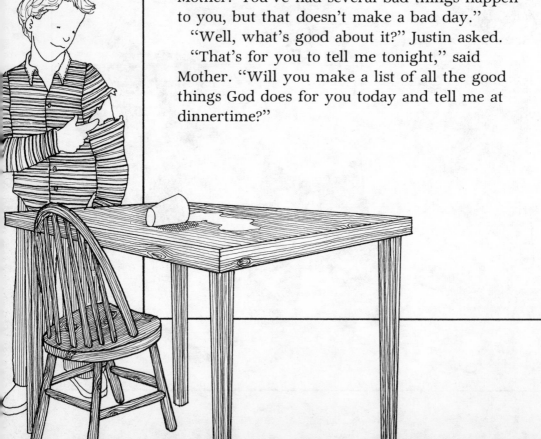

Justin thought that would be fun. By dinner-time the list was quite long. There were a few more bad things on the list, but there were many more good things that God had done for him.

"This really was a good day after all," said Justin. "It was a good day with a few bad things in it."

A Little Talk about God and You

1. Why did Justin's bad day become a good day? What made the difference?
2. How many good things do you think God does for you each day? Would you like to talk about some of the good things God did for you today?

BIBLE READING: Psalm 118:24.
BIBLE TRUTH: This is a day the Lord has made. Let us rejoice and be glad in it. From Psalm 118:24.
PRAYER: Dear God, when I think I'm having a bad day, remind me to count the good things You give me. Then I will remember that I am having a good day because of You. Amen.

Good Things:
1. Sara said "Hello" t
2. We didn't have a test
3. Bob gave me half of
4. I got to ride in Aunt C
5. Tom came over after s
6. I found my violin I'd left
7. We had a field trip in Sch
8. The dentist said "Good bru
9. Mrs. Triolo gave me $5.00 for
10. I got all my reading finishe
11. I only missed two answers in
12. Tina's cat had kittens and I get
13. Dad promised to take me to th
14. Gordy and I got to build a skate b
15. We are having spaghetti for dinner
16. Lindsay is giving me her old baseball
17. Taylor got his first tooth in today
18. Mom bought me new purple high tops
19. Mr. Caldwell fixed my bike tire for free
20. Steven and I got to trade desserts too
21. My teacher asked me to read out loud to
22. I got to sit by Sara during the assembly
23.
24.

God Was Here First!

"Doesn't our neighbor across the street ever go to church?" Adam asked Father.

"No, he says he doesn't believe there is a God," said Father. "So why go to worship and sing about a Person who isn't there?"

"But what do you say to him about that?" Adam asked.

What would you say to Adam's neighbor?

A Little Talk about Believing in God

1. Do you know someone who says there is no God?
2. What should Christians say to a person like that?
3. What do you think God would say to a person like that?

"I read chapters 38 and 39 of Job to him," said Father. "God gives a long list of the wonderful things that only God could do."

"What are some of those things?" Adam asked.

"Oh, special things like making the world, putting the oceans where they should be, and opening and closing the gates of life and death," said Father.

"Wow, I guess our neighbor can't do any of those things, can he?" Adam asked.

"No one but God can do these things," said Father. "If you look at the things God made, you have to know that God is the One who made them."

A Little Talk about God and You

1. Can you make a sunset or a cloud? Can you put the oceans in their places? Can you control life and death?
2. Who is the only Person who can do these things? Can you see the things that God has made and not believe that God made them?

BIBLE READING: Job 38 and 39.
BIBLE TRUTH: Where were you when God made the earth? He was there! Were you? From Job 38:4.
PRAYER: Dear God, I know You are there, even though I can't see You. I see all the wonderful things You have made, and I know that only You could make them. Thank You for being a wonderful God. Amen.

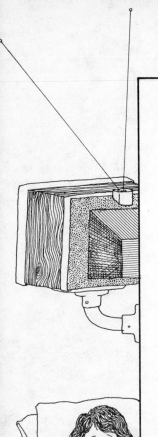

A Special Friend Is with You

"I'm scared," said Blair. "Don't leave me alone in this hospital."

Mother smiled and put Blair's hand in hers.

"Someone very important is going to stay with you in this hospital tonight," said Father.

"Who?" Blair asked. "Is it the doctor who will take out my tonsils?"

"No, it is Someone much more important than the doctor," said Father.

Do you know who this special Friend is?

A Little Talk about a Special Friend

1. Have you ever stayed at a hospital? How long were you there? Were you glad for the nurses and doctors? They are special friends, aren't they?
2. Do you think another special Friend was there with you? Who was He?

"Do not be afraid, for I am with you," said Father. "That's what God says in Isaiah 43:5. He is the most special Friend of all. He will be with you, right here by your bed, every minute tonight. And He will stay with you tomorrow, too."

Blair thought about that for a long time. "I wish you could be here with me too," she said. "But I won't be afraid now, because I know that God is with me, right here in this room."

A Little Talk about God and You

1. The next time you are lonely or afraid, remember that God is there with you. Talk with Him. Tell Him that You love Him. Thank Him for being your Friend.
2. Is there anyone bigger than God? Is there anyone stronger than God? If God is with you, why should you be afraid of anything else?

BIBLE READING: Isaiah 43:1-5.
BIBLE TRUTH: Do not be afraid, for I am with you. From Isaiah 43:5.
PRAYER: Dear God, thank You for staying with me when I am alone. Help me not to be afraid, for You will take care of me. Amen.

LITTLE TALK 54

God's Record Book

"That's three times you have used that bad word today," Mother told Al. "Should I make a chart on the wall that shows all the bad words you use?"

Al thought about a chart on the wall. He could see it there. "Al's Bad Words," it would say. Or it might say, "All the Bad Things Al Has Done." That would be worse.

"I don't think I would like a chart that shows all the bad things I do," Al said.

"And neither would I," said Mother. "I would not want God to make a chart like that for me."

A Little Talk about God's Records

1. Would you like a chart on the wall that shows all the bad things you have done? Would you want all your friends to come in and read it? Why not?
2. Would you want God to put up a chart like that? Would you want Him to list all the bad things you have done? Why not?

"Does God keep a chart like that?" Al asked Mother. "Would He show it to everyone?"

"God knows everything," said Mother. "So He knows everything we have done wrong. But when we ask Him to forgive us, we ask Him to forget all those bad things."

"Does He?" Al asked.

"That's what the Bible tells us," said Mother. Then she read Jeremiah 31:34. Would you like to read that?

A Little Talk about God and You

1. Do you want God to forgive you for the bad things you have said or done? Why?
2. When God forgives you, does He also forget the bad things you have done? How do you know?
3. Why should you forgive others when they ask you? Why should you forget the bad things they have done against you? What would Jesus want you to do?

BIBLE READING: Psalm 130:3.

BIBLE TRUTH: God says, "I will forgive their sins and remember them no more." From Jeremiah 31:34.

PRAYER: Thank You, dear God, for forgetting my sins when You forgive me, and for not keeping a chart of my sins in Your house. Amen.

Will I Have Enough if I Give?

"These poor people really need help," said Lauren. She pointed to a picture of some starving people in Africa.

"Yes, they certainly do," said Mother. "We give some money to an organization that helps feed them. Many people do."

"You and Father give a lot of money to things like this, don't you?" Lauren asked. "Do you ever give too much? I mean, do you give so much that we don't have any left over?"

A Little Talk about Giving

1. Why should we give money to help poor people? Would it be better to keep the money and have fun with it?
2. If we give money to help poor people, will we have enough to feed ourselves?

"We give to help God's work," said Mother. "Part of God's work is to help poor people."

"Will we still have enough for our house and food?" asked Lauren.

"Yes, we have always had enough, and more," said Mother. "We must pay our bills, of course." Then Mother read Proverbs 28:27 to Lauren. Would you like to read that too?

A Little Talk about God and You

1. Which would please God more, for you to be generous or stingy? Why?
2. Which kind of person would God rather give to? Why? Which kind of person would you rather be? Why?

BIBLE READING: Proverbs 28:25-27.
BIBLE TRUTH: A person who gives to the poor will always have plenty left over. But a person who ignores the poor won't do so well. From Proverbs 28:27.
PRAYER: Dear God, I want to help others who can't help themselves. I know that's what You want Your people to do. Amen.

Hush! Be Still!

"Hush! Be still!" said Mother. Arlene was very quiet. Then she heard the sweet song of a bird outside her window.

"Shhh! Be quiet!" said Father. Arlene was very still. Then she heard the wind sighing in the trees.

"Listen!" said Mother. Arlene listened carefully. Then she heard the rumble of thunder.

"Do you hear it?" Father asked. Arlene listened. She heard the soft patter of the rain falling on her windowpane.

Do you like lots of noise? Or do you like to be quiet and hear something special?

A Little Talk about Being Quiet

1. How many special things did Arlene hear when she was quiet?
2. When you walk outside, stop and listen. Count how many different special sounds you hear.

"We hear better when we are quiet," said Father. "There is a time for noise, and there is a time to be quiet so we can listen."

"I'm glad I was quiet so I could hear these special sounds," said Arlene.

"We need to be quiet when we want to be with God, too," said Father. "It's easier to listen to His Word and pray to Him and think about Him when we are quiet."

A Little Talk about God and You

1. Have you read the Bible today, or has someone read it to you? Is it easier to listen to God's Word when you are quiet or when you are noisy?
2. Have you prayed today? Is it easier to talk to God when you are quiet or when you are noisy?
3. Have you sat quietly thinking about God today? Is it easier to think about God when you are quiet or when you are noisy?

BIBLE READING: Psalm 46:7-11.
BIBLE TRUTH: Be still and know that I am God. From Psalm 46:10.
PRAYER: Dear God, I want to sit quietly with You and think about You and talk with You. Be with me now as I do this. Amen.

Who Will Know?

Two boys were on their way to Sunday school. Their parents had given each of them a quarter for the offering.

"Let's stop here at the drugstore to buy some candy with our quarters," said the first boy. "No one will ever know."

A Little Talk about What God Sees

1. Do you think this boy is right? Will anyone know what they did?
2. What would you say if you were the other boy?

"But Someone very important will know as soon as we do it," said the second boy.

The first boy looked surprised. "Our parents won't see us," he said. "Our Sunday school teacher won't see us. And our pastor won't see us. Who else will see us?"

"God will see us," said the second boy. "He sees everything we do, so He will see us do this. No, I'm going to put my quarter in the offering plate for Him."

A Little Talk about God and You

1. Do you think the second boy is right? Does God see everything we do?
2. If we have an offering for God, why should we not buy candy with it? Can you think of two or three good reasons?
3. Check your answers with these: 1) I give to God because I love Him; 2) I give to God because He has given so much to me; 3) I give to God because what I have really belongs to Him; 4) I give to God because I want to help His friends do His work; 5) I give to God to take care of His house.

BIBLE READING: Proverbs 5:21,22.
BIBLE TRUTH: Your ways are clearly seen by the Lord. From Proverbs 5:21.
PRAYER: Dear God, I will give to please You. May I do what is right because I love You, not just because You will see me do something wrong. Amen.

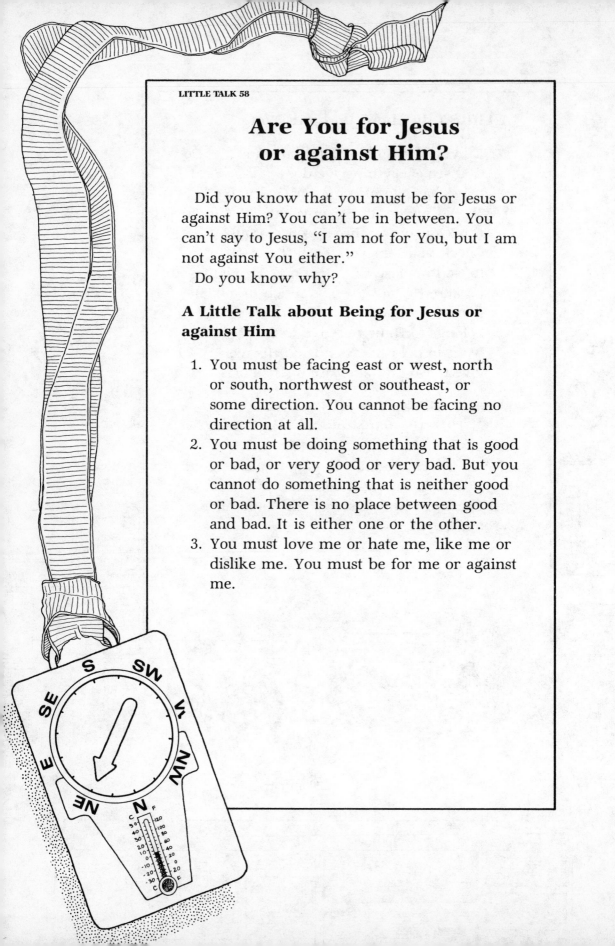

Are You for Jesus or against Him?

Did you know that you must be for Jesus or against Him? You can't be in between. You can't say to Jesus, "I am not for You, but I am not against You either."

Do you know why?

A Little Talk about Being for Jesus or against Him

1. You must be facing east or west, north or south, northwest or southeast, or some direction. You cannot be facing no direction at all.

2. You must be doing something that is good or bad, or very good or very bad. But you cannot do something that is neither good or bad. There is no place between good and bad. It is either one or the other.

3. You must love me or hate me, like me or dislike me. You must be for me or against me.

Have you ever tried to face no direction at all? You can't, can you? Have you ever tried doing something that is neither good nor bad? You can't, can you? Have you ever tried to keep from moving at all?

Jesus said that you must either be for Him or against Him. You can't be in the middle.

A Little Talk about Jesus and You

1. Do you love Jesus? You must either love Him or not love Him. You cannot be in between.
2. Have you asked Jesus to be your Savior? He is either your Savior or He isn't. There is no place in between.
3. Are you trying to live the way Jesus wants you to? You must either live the way He wants you to or live the way He doesn't want. There is no other way.

BIBLE READING: Matthew 12:30.
BIBLE TRUTH: Jesus said, "A person must be for me or against me." There is no other way. From Matthew 12:30.
PRAYER: Dear Jesus, I don't want to be against You, so I want to be for You. I don't want to hate You, so I want to love You. I don't want to displease You, so I want to please You. Amen.

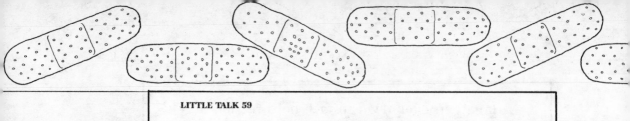

Ten Fingers

"Let me put a Band-Aid on your finger," said Mother. "That will keep the dirt from the place where you cut your finger."

Kristi was still sniffling when Mother finished. It was no fun to cut a finger.

"But I can't play the piano now," said Kristi.

Mother smiled. "Have you tried to play the piano with your elbow?" she asked. "Or what about your toes?"

Kristi smiled too. She thought it would look quite funny to play the piano with her elbows or toes.

"God made fingers to help us do special things," said Mother. "Can you think of other special things that your fingers can do?"

A Little Talk about Fingers

1. What can you do with your fingers that you can't do with your elbows or toes?
2. Make a list of the special things that you like to do with your fingers. How many will you do today?

Kristi made a list of things that she did with her fingers. "I button my blouse and coat with my fingers," she said. "I can't do that with my elbow or toes. I hold my pencil while I write. I also pet my dog and cat with my fingers. And I hold my spoon and fork with my fingers when I eat."

"Then we should thank God for your fingers," said Mother. So they did.

A Little Talk about God and You

1. Who made your fingers? Have you ever thought of the things you could not do if you did not have fingers? Look at the list you made.
2. Have you ever thanked God for your fingers? Why not do that now?

BIBLE READING: Psalm 90:16,17.
BIBLE TRUTH: Help us do well with the work of our hands. From Psalm 90:17.
PRAYER: Dear God, thank You for fingers to do good things. May I use them to honor You. Amen.

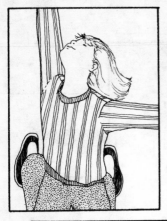

Who Do You Trust?

"I don't trust anyone except my family and friends," said one man.

"I don't trust anyone except myself," said a second man.

"I don't trust anyone," said a third man.

"You all forgot Someone you can trust at any time," said a fourth man. Who is this?

A Little Talk about Trusting

1. Have you ever thought that you can't trust anyone but yourself? Is that really true?
2. Think of some people you can trust.

The fourth man told the others about a special verse in the Bible. "Trust in the Lord and do good," he said. "That is from Psalm 37:3. God will never do anything to hurt you. He will always give you good things to eat. He will always take care of you. He will always keep His promises. He will always tell the truth."

If you knew someone else like that, would you trust him?

A Little Talk about God and You

1. What are some good reasons why you can always trust God? Are these the same reasons why you trust other people? Are these the same reasons why others trust you?
2. Why are you glad that you can always trust God? How would you feel if you could never trust Him?

BIBLE READING: Psalm 37:3.

BIBLE TRUTH: Trust in the Lord and do good. From Psalm 37:3.

PRAYER: Thank You, dear God, that I can trust You. I want to live so that my friends and family can trust me, too. Amen.

Will You Cry with Me?

Your best friend Bert hurt his finger. It hurts so much that he cries. Should you feel sad with him or should you feel glad?

Brandon doesn't like you and has tried to hurt you many times. He hurts his finger. It hurts so much that he cries. Should you feel sad with him or should you feel glad?

Bert gets a new bike for his birthday. You have wanted a new bike for such a long time, but you did not get one. Your parents don't have the money to buy it. Should you feel glad with Bert?

Brandon gets a new bike too. Should you feel glad with Brandon?

A Little Talk about Laughing and Crying

1. Should we be glad when friends get good things? Why? Should we be sad when friends hurt? Why?
2. Should we be glad when people who are mean to us get good things? Should we be sad when people who are mean to us get hurt?

Bert is a friend. Of course you are glad when he gets something good. You should even be glad when he gets something good that you can't get.

And when Bert hurts, you hurt too, don't you? That's because you and Bert are friends.

But how about Brandon, who sometimes makes you cry? When he hurts his finger, should you be glad? What would Jesus do? If Brandon gets something good that you can't get, what should you do? What would Jesus do?

A Little Talk about Jesus and You

1. Would Jesus laugh when an enemy got hurt? No, Jesus would hurt with him. Would Jesus be glad when an enemy got something good? Yes, He would.
2. When we follow Jesus, why should we do what Jesus would do? This means that we should be sad when Brandon gets hurt and glad when he gets a new bike, doesn't it?

BIBLE READING: Romans 12:15.
BIBLE TRUTH: Be glad with others who are glad, and sad with others who are sad. From Romans 12:15.
PRAYER: Dear Jesus, teach me to do what You would do. When others hurt, may I hurt with them. When others are glad, may I be glad with them. Amen.

Are You Rich or Poor?

Once there were two men. One had all the rich food that money could buy. He had a big table and many servants to bring his food to him. He ate his food on silver plates and drank from gold cups. This man often grumbled because his food was not served fast enough, or in the way he thought it should be served, or because of some other little problem. This man did not even seem grateful for his food. He never stopped to thank God for it.

The other man did not have rich food. But he always seemed to have enough, and it was good food. This man was thankful for his food. Before he ate, he always thanked God for his food. He and his family talked about happy things while they ate.

A Little Talk about Thankfulness

1. Which family would you rather eat with tonight? Why? Why would you rather not eat with the other family?
2. What must you do to have a happy mealtime? Do you do these things?

The rich man had more than enough food, and better food than he needed. But he was not happy. He always wanted more, and better, and faster. He wasn't even thankful, and never told God how grateful he was for

his rich food. So what did he have that you would want except a little fancier food?

The other man had enough food, and it was good, and he told God how thankful he was. He also made it fun to eat at his table. Of course you would rather eat at his table, wouldn't you?

The amount of food is not as important as the amount of thankfulness we have for our food. The richness of the food is not as important as the fun we have eating it. It is not as important to have everything done my way as to know that everything is being done God's way.

A Little Talk about God and You

1. Would you rather have God or this rich man at your dinner table tonight? God will be there if you invite Him. The rich man would not come even if you invited him.
2. Would you rather have less food and more fun? Would you rather have more ordinary food and be thankful for it? Would you like to thank God for your food now?

BIBLE READING: Proverbs 15:15-17.
BIBLE TRUTH: It is better to eat an ordinary meal with love than a rich banquet with hatred. From Proverbs 15:17.
PRAYER: Dear God, help me to be grateful for dinner tonight, no matter what I have on my plate. Amen.

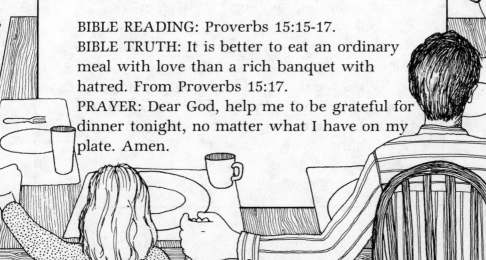

Gifts Too Good to Forget

"Did you hear that Mr. Hanson is giving a new organ to our church?" Father said at dinner one evening.

"Oh, that's wonderful," said Mother. "We need a new organ. But why is he giving such a wonderful gift?"

"He wants us to remember the beautiful way his wife sang when she was living," said Father. "The organ will help us do that."

A Little Talk about Special Gifts

1. Why does Mr. Hanson want to give the organ to the church? Why will this organ be a special gift?
2. How will the organ help people remember Mrs. Hanson's singing?

"Mrs. Hanson was one of our best singers," said Mother. "Every time I heard her, I thought about the beautiful voice God gave her."

"Now every time we hear the organ we will think about her singing," said Father.

"And we will think about God's special gifts to us, such as Mrs. Hanson's voice," said Mother.

"When we think about God's special gifts, we should thank Him for them," said Father. "So why don't we thank God now for this special organ?"

A Little Talk about God and You

1. Why should we thank God for a beautiful voice that sings songs about Him? Why should we thank God for special gifts like the organ?
2. What special gifts has God given to you? Would you like to thank Him for them now?

BIBLE READING: James 1:17.
BIBLE TRUTH: Every good and perfect gift comes from God. From James 1:17.
PRAYER: Dear God, thank You for good gifts. Thank You most of all for the good gifts You have given me. Amen.

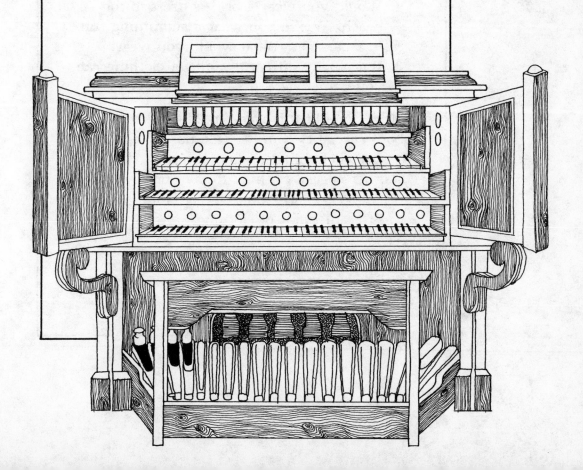

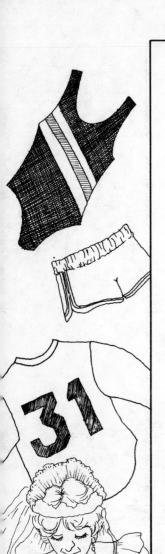

What Kind of Clothes Do You Have?

"Look at that beautiful bride's dress," Teri said to her Aunt Sue.

Aunt Sue smiled. "Would you like to wear one like that someday?" she asked.

"Oh, yes," said Teri.

"Would you wear it to play baseball?" Aunt Sue asked.

Teri laughed. "People wear baseball uniforms to play baseball," she said.

"And football uniforms to play football?" Aunt Sue asked. "Let's make a list of all the different kinds of clothing that we wear."

A Little Talk about Clothing

1. Would you wear a bride's dress to the beach? Would you wear a swimming suit to a banquet? What would you wear?
2. How many different kinds of clothing can you name?

Teri thought this was fun. She talked about special clothing to ride horses, and other special clothing to play tennis, and still other special clothing to play hockey. Before long, Teri and Aunt Sue had a long list of different kinds of clothing.

"There's one we haven't put on the list yet," said Aunt Sue. "It's called the garments of salvation."

Then Aunt Sue read Isaiah 61:10 to Teri. "Have you ever heard of garments of salvation?" Aunt Sue asked Teri. "You can't see them, but God puts them on us when we become His people. When we accept Jesus as our Savior, we receive salvation from God. God calls salvation a special kind of clothing."

"That sounds even more special than a bride's dress," said Teri. "I'm glad I'm wearing these beautiful clothes, even though I can't see them."

A Little Talk about God and You

1. Have you ever asked Jesus to be your Savior? If you have, God has put the "garments of salvation" on you.
2. You can't see these special clothes, but you can thank God for them. Would you like to do that now?

BIBLE READING: Isaiah 61:10.
BIBLE TRUTH: God lets me wear the garments of salvation. This is like a bridegroom or bride dressing up for a wedding. From Isaiah 61:10.
PRAYER: Thank You, dear God, for these beautiful clothes of salvation. I know I can't see them, but it helps just to know they are there. Amen.

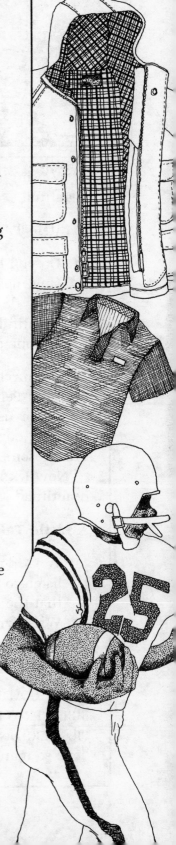

Singing for the Lord

"I liked the singing this morning in church," said Adele. "When the angels sing, it must sound something like that."

Father smiled. "I've never heard angels sing," he said. "But if I did, they probably would sound like the people of our church."

"We sing songs at school, but they don't sound that beautiful," said Adele. "Why not?"

A Little Talk about Singing

1. Do you like to sing? What kind of songs do you like to sing most?
2. Why do you think the songs at church seem more beautiful to Adele? Have you ever thought that the songs at your church seem more beautiful than others?

"At church we sing about God," said Father. "He is a beautiful Person to sing about. He has done many beautiful things for us and has given many beautiful things to us. We also sing our songs *to* God. We are praising Him as we sing. That is something beautiful to do."

"Now I know why the songs at church sound more beautiful," said Adele.

A Little Talk about God and You

1. What do the songs at church tell you about God? Do you listen to the words and learn about Him as you sing? Try that the next time you sing at church.
2. When you sing at church, are you singing to God? Are you praising Him as you sing? Remember that the next time you sing.

BIBLE READING: Exodus 15:1,2.
BIBLE TRUTH: Sing praises to God. From Psalm 47:6.
PRAYER: Dear God, I will praise You as I sing, for You have done so many wonderful things for me. Amen.

What Happens When Mother Gets Sick?

Mother almost never gets sick. But sometimes it happens, and today was one of those times.

"What will we do?" Barbara asked.

"How will we get something to eat?" asked Barbara's father.

"Who will wash the dishes and make the beds?" asked Barbara's brother.

Who do you think will do all these things?

A Little Talk about Helping

1. Make a list of all the things that Mother does for you each day. Talk with Mother about your list and see if you remembered most things.
2. Have you thanked Mother for all she does for you?
3. What would you like to say to Barbara about doing Mother's work when she is sick? What do you think Barbara and her family will do?

"I will cook breakfast and dinner," said Father.

"I will make the lunches for us to take to school," said Barbara.

"I will help clean the house," said Barbara's brother.

"And we will all wash and dry the dishes together," said Father. "Then we will tell Mother how thankful we are for all she does for us."

A Little Talk about Jesus and You

1. Do you think Barbara and her family are pleasing Jesus? Why?
2. What would Jesus say to people who would not help their own family? What would you say to them?

BIBLE READING: Matthew 25:35,36.
BIBLE TRUTH: I was sick and you looked after me. From Matthew 25:36.
PRAYER: Dear Jesus, You helped so many people who were sick and needed You. Please teach me to help others who are sick, especially my own family. Amen.

Sweet Things

"This candy is so sweet," a girl said to her father.

"This syrup on my pancakes is so sweet," a boy said to his mother.

"This honey is so sweet," a girl said to her brother.

"This chewing gum is so sweet," a boy said to his sister.

"This Bible verse is so sweet," Mother said. What do you think Mother meant?

A Little Talk about Sweetness

1. Can you think of several things that are sweet? Would you rather eat something sweet than something bitter? Why? Why do you think people don't make salty ice cream or bitter candy?

2. If you could think of a good taste for a Bible verse, would you think of it as bitter, salty, or sweet? Why?

"How sweet are your promises to my taste, sweeter than honey to my mouth!" Mother read. "This is from Psalm 119:103."

"Sweeter than candy and honey?" the girl asked.

"Sweeter than syrup and chewing gum?" the boy asked.

"That's what the Bible says," Mother answered.

"No wonder we get hungry to read the Bible and listen to it," said Father.

This family decided to have a little sweetness, so they sat down and read the Bible together.

A Little Talk about God and You

1. Since God's Word is sweet, wouldn't you like it more often?
2. Are you glad that God made His Word sweet, not bitter? Have you thanked God for His Word? Would you like to do that now?

BIBLE READING: Psalm 119:102-104.
BIBLE TRUTH: Your Word is sweet, even sweeter than honey. From Psalm 119:103.
PRAYER: Dear God, thank You for Your Word. Thank You for making it sweet, so that I want it. I'm glad it is not like bitter medicine. Amen.

Treasure

Long ago a king had a room full of gold. The king often went to the room to look at his gold. He picked up his gold and touched it. He loved his gold. The king would give up almost anything rather than his gold.

Not long ago a man had a lot of things. He spent more time with his things than he did with his wife and children.

What do you think is wrong with these men?

A Little Talk about Treasure

1. Why do we need money? What do we do with it? Do you need 20 million dollars? How much do you need?
2. The Bible says that our heart is where our treasure is. This means that people often love money too much. They want more money than they need. What would you say to people like that?

One day the king saw a poor widow. The poor woman did not have enough to eat. He felt sorry for this widow. He decided to give her one gold coin.

The woman now had enough money to buy food for a long time. She was so thankful. This made the king very happy. He was surprised. He found that he was happier giving a gold coin away than keeping it. Why do you think the king felt this way?

A Little Talk about Jesus and You

1. Did Jesus have a lot of money? Why do you think He never sat in a room, counting His gold or silver? What did He think was more important?
2. The Bible does not tell us that it is wrong to have enough money. But it does tell us that we should not love money more than God, or our family, or the really important things.

BIBLE READING: 1 Timothy 6:10.
BIBLE TRUTH: Where your treasure is, your heart will be also. From Matthew 6:21.
PRAYER: Dear Jesus, thank You for telling me what is most important. May I never love money more than You, but always put the really important things in life first. Amen.

Who Made This Mess?

"Oh, no!" Mother said as she walked into the living room. "Look at my yarn! It's a terrible mess."

Mother looked at Betsy's baby brother. "I should not have left you alone with my yarn," she said. "Now you have made such a mess with it."

But it was not Betsy's brother who had done this. Betsy had done it when she looked through Mother's knitting basket.

Betsy was glad that Mother did not think she did it. She was glad that Mother thought her little brother had done it.

Betsy started outside. She looked back at Mother. She could see that Mother was angry at her little brother.

Suddenly Betsy felt sad. She did not want Mother to be angry at her little brother. But then she did not want Mother to be angry at her, either. What should she do?

A Little Talk about Telling the Truth

1. Why do you think Betsy felt sad? Would you like to see your little brother blamed for something you did wrong? Why not?
2. What would you tell Betsy she should do?

Betsy went back into the living room. She looked at Mother and thought she would cry.

"Mother, I was the one who messed up your yarn," she said. "I'm really sorry."

Mother smiled and gave Betsy a big hug. "I'm sorry you messed up my yarn," she said. "But I'm very glad you told me about it. Thank you for being an honest girl."

A Little Talk about Jesus and You

1. Read John 14:6. Who said He is truth? Would Jesus ever tell a lie or be dishonest with someone? Why not?
2. When we love Jesus, should we tell a lie or be dishonest? Why not? Why would Jesus be hurt if we tell a lie or are dishonest with other people?
3. Will you remember this the next time you are tempted to tell a lie or be dishonest?

BIBLE READING: Philippians 4:8,9.
BIBLE TRUTH: Think about things that are true and right, pure and lovely. From Philippians 4:8.
PRAYER: Dear Jesus, it's so easy to tell a little lie or do something that is not honest. But I want to be more like You, and I know You would not do any of these things. Amen.

Where Do Hurtful Words Come From?

"That boy should have his mouth washed out with soap," a lady said. The boy had said some words that were not very nice. The lady did not like to hear them.

"No, that wouldn't do any good," said another lady. "He should have his heart washed out instead."

A Little Talk about Mouths and Hearts

1. What did this second lady mean, that the boy should have his heart washed out?
2. Where do hurtful words come from first, the mouth or the heart?

"The Bible says that words which come out of our mouths come from our hearts first," the second lady said. "That boy's mouth is just saying what his heart wants it to say."

Which should be cleaned first, the boy's heart or his mouth?

A Little Talk about God and You

1. Can you wash your mouth? When you do, does it keep you from saying things you should not say?
2. Who can wash or clean your heart? Can you do that by yourself? Can God do it for you? When He does, will He help you stop saying things you should not say?

BIBLE READING: Matthew 15:17-20.
BIBLE TRUTH: Words that come from the mouth come first from the heart. Bad thoughts come from the heart. From Matthew 15:18,19.
PRAYER: Dear God, when I want to say hurtful words or words that would not please You, please clean my heart so that my mouth will say the right things. Amen.

THINK ABOUT IT IN YOUR HEART
BEFORE YOU SAY IT!

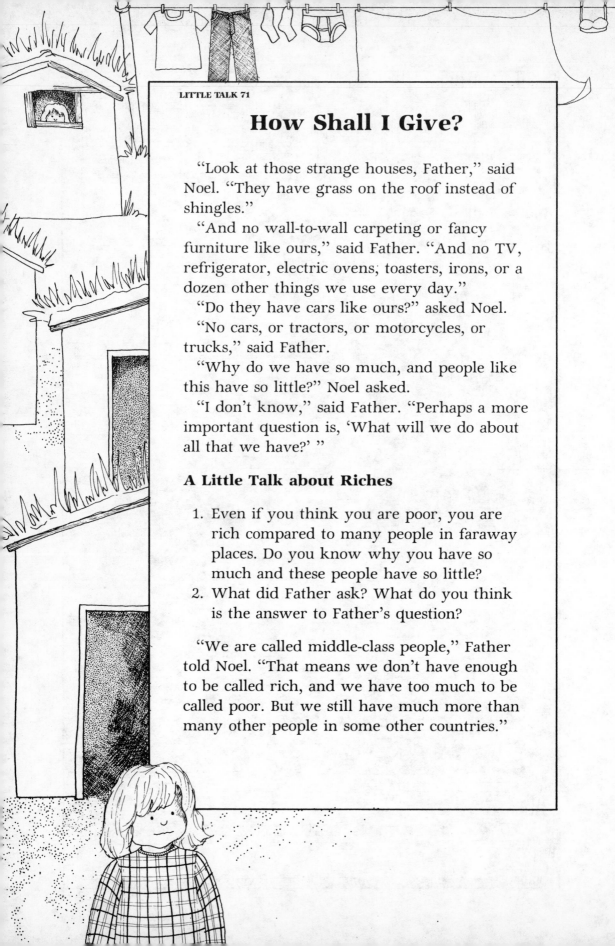

How Shall I Give?

"Look at those strange houses, Father," said Noel. "They have grass on the roof instead of shingles."

"And no wall-to-wall carpeting or fancy furniture like ours," said Father. "And no TV, refrigerator, electric ovens, toasters, irons, or a dozen other things we use every day."

"Do they have cars like ours?" asked Noel.

"No cars, or tractors, or motorcycles, or trucks," said Father.

"Why do we have so much, and people like this have so little?" Noel asked.

"I don't know," said Father. "Perhaps a more important question is, 'What will we do about all that we have?' "

A Little Talk about Riches

1. Even if you think you are poor, you are rich compared to many people in faraway places. Do you know why you have so much and these people have so little?
2. What did Father ask? What do you think is the answer to Father's question?

"We are called middle-class people," Father told Noel. "That means we don't have enough to be called rich, and we have too much to be called poor. But we still have much more than many other people in some other countries."

"You asked what we should do with all that we have," said Noel. "What should we do? Should we give it all away?"

Father smiled. "If we did that, then we would be poor and others would have to help take care of us," he said. "No, God does not ask us to give it all away, only some of it. But we must give part of what we have to help God's work and God's people. When we do that, it's the same as giving to God."

"How much should we give?" asked Noel.

"How much have we received?" asked Father. "The more God gives us, the more we should give."

A Little Talk about God and You

1. Has God given you and your family many good things? Has He given you much or little?
2. This helps you know how much to give God's work and God's people. If He has given much, you should give much too.

BIBLE READING: Luke 6:38.
BIBLE TRUTH: Freely you have received, freely give. From Matthew 10:8.
PRAYER: Dear God, You have given generously. Help me not to be stingy when I give to You. Amen.

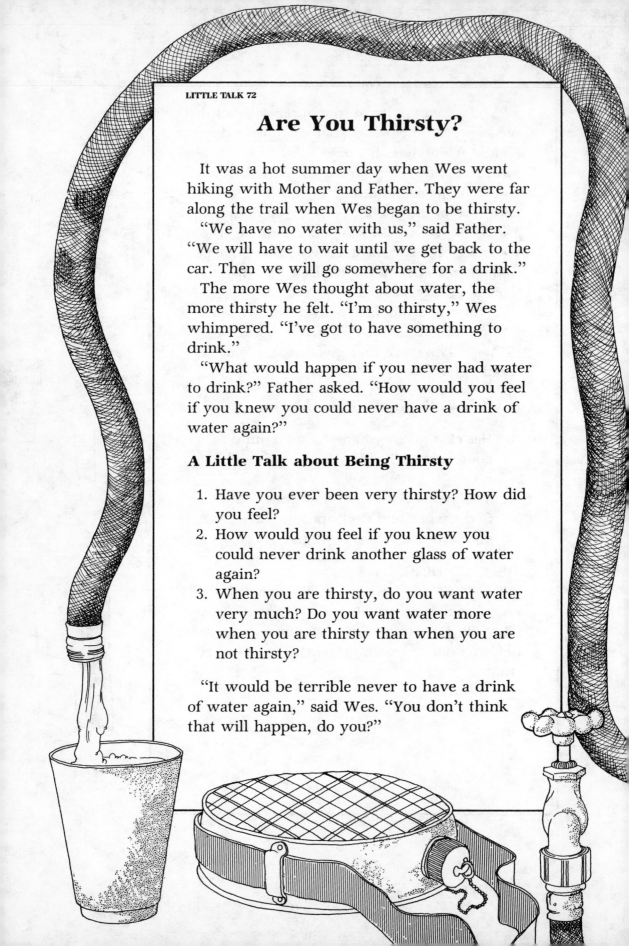

Are You Thirsty?

It was a hot summer day when Wes went hiking with Mother and Father. They were far along the trail when Wes began to be thirsty.

"We have no water with us," said Father. "We will have to wait until we get back to the car. Then we will go somewhere for a drink."

The more Wes thought about water, the more thirsty he felt. "I'm so thirsty," Wes whimpered. "I've got to have something to drink."

"What would happen if you never had water to drink?" Father asked. "How would you feel if you knew you could never have a drink of water again?"

A Little Talk about Being Thirsty

1. Have you ever been very thirsty? How did you feel?
2. How would you feel if you knew you could never drink another glass of water again?
3. When you are thirsty, do you want water very much? Do you want water more when you are thirsty than when you are not thirsty?

"It would be terrible never to have a drink of water again," said Wes. "You don't think that will happen, do you?"

Father laughed. "No, we'll get some water before long," he said. "But some people are thirsty for God all their lives but never let God satisfy their thirst."

"Is that why so many people hurt like I do now?" Wes asked.

"Yes," said Father. "When we thirst for God, we don't feel good until we let God satisfy our thirst. He is the only One who can take that thirsty feeling away."

A Little Talk about God and You

1. Have you ever wanted God to do something special for you? You were thirsting for Him.
2. Have you ever wanted to talk to God about something? Have you ever hoped God would be with you when you were lonely or afraid? You were thirsting for Him.

BIBLE READING: Psalm 42:1,2.
BIBLE TRUTH: My soul thirsts for God. From Psalm 42:2. Jesus said, "Whoever drinks the water I give him will never thirst." From John 4:14.
PRAYER: Dear God, whenever I get thirsty, I will remember that I need You more than water. Amen.

GRATEFUL   LOVE   TRUST   MERCY

HUMBLE

SELF CONTROL

WAIT

OBEDIENT

KINDNESS

GOOD

PRAY

DILIGENT

GENEROUS

STRAIGHT

GLAD

LITTLE TALK 73

If I Were God

"If I were God, I would hit that man every day for the rest of his life," said Jim.

"Why?" asked Mother.

"Because he hit his wife and made her go to the hospital," said Jim.

Do you think Jim is right? Would this be the best way to punish that man?

A Little Talk about God's Ways and Our Ways

1. Why did Jim think God should hit that man every day? Do you think God should do that?

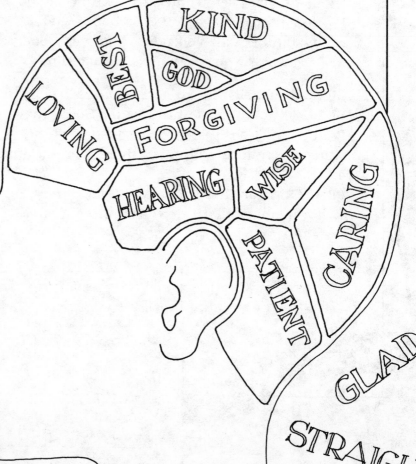

2. Would you like to change some ways that God does things? Which ways? Why?

"Did you know that this man became a Christian in prison?" Mother asked. "He has changed completely. Now he is helping other people know Jesus."

"Did God forgive him?" Jim asked.

"Yes," said Mother. "Would you still like to have God hit him every day?"

Jim thought of this man telling people about Jesus. He thought about the way the man had changed.

"I guess God knows how to handle these things better than I do," said Jim.

A Little Talk about God and You

1. Would you like God to think exactly the way you do? Why not?
2. What are some things that God would not have done if He had thought the way you think? Would He have made a world? Would He forgive sin? Would He have given us the Bible, His Word?

BIBLE READING: Isaiah 55:8,9.

BIBLE TRUTH: "My ways are not your ways," says the Lord. "My ways are much higher than your ways." From Isaiah 55:9.

PRAYER: Teach me, dear God, to do things the way You would do them. And please don't do things the way I would do them. Amen.

I Can't Do That

Alex was trying to learn a new Bible verse. It wasn't an easy one to learn, so Alex gave up.

"I can't do it," he said.

"You cannot or you will not?" Grandpa asked.

"What's the difference?" Alex asked.

A Little Talk about Can't

1. Think of some things that you really can't do, such as jump over a building, fly by flapping your arms, or memorize the whole Bible in an hour.
2. Do you think Alex cannot or will not learn this one Bible verse? How would you explain the difference to Alex?

"Tell me some things you really can't do," said Grandpa.

Alex thought about this. "I can't swim across the ocean, I can't dig a hole all the way through the earth, and I can't disappear," he said.

"Very good!" said Grandpa. "Now, is learning one Bible verse one of those kinds of things?"

Alex thought again. He had learned many Bible verses. He knew he could learn this one if he worked long enough and hard enough.

"I *can* learn this Bible verse," Alex said. "And I *will*!"

A Little Talk about God and You

1. Is there anything that God can't do? Why is this true?
2. Are there some things you can't do? Why can't you do anything you want to do? Are there some things you think you can't do, but you really can? Why not ask God to help you?

BIBLE READING: Matthew 19:26.
BIBLE TRUTH: People can't do some things, but God can do anything. From Matthew 19:26.
PRAYER: Dear God, teach me to know what I really can't do, and what I shouldn't do. And help me to know what I can do and what I should do. Then show me how to do what You want me to do. Amen.

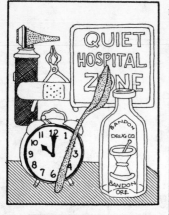

Who Heals You?

"This medicine healed me," said a man one day. "As soon as I took the medicine, it made me well."

"I have a good doctor," said a woman one day. "He healed me when I got sick."

"That was a wonderful hospital," said another man. "They healed me when I was hurt."

"When I got sick, I didn't go to a doctor, or take medicine, or go to a hospital," said another woman. "I let my body heal itself."

Which of these people is right?

A Little Talk about Healing

1. Does medicine heal us? Do doctors or hospitals heal us? Do our bodies heal themselves?

2. When you are healed, how does it happen? Who does it?

"It was I who healed them," the Lord said one day (Hosea 11:3). The Lord was healing people different from us. He was healing something different from a cut finger. But it was the Lord who was healing.

All healing comes from the Lord. Only the One who made you can heal you. Medicine may help, doctors may help, hospitals may help, and even our own bodies may help. But only the Lord can heal.

A Little Talk about Jesus and You

1. Should we take medicines to help us get well? Should we ask doctors to help us get well? Should we go to a hospital when we get very sick?

2. What else should we do before we use the best medicines, doctors, and hospitals? Do you remember to pray and ask Jesus to heal you?

BIBLE READING: Matthew 14:35,36.

BIBLE TRUTH: It is God who heals us. From Hosea 11:3.

PRAYER: Dear Jesus, I thank You for good medicines, good doctors, and good hospitals. But most of all I thank You for healing my body when I am sick or hurt. Amen.

Read, Learn, and Do

Casey reads his Bible each day. He wants to know what God says in His Word.

Jackie reads her Bible each day too. But she asks Mother or Father what it means. She wants to know what the Bible says, but she also wants to know what it means.

Damon reads his Bible each day too. He also asks Mother or Father what it means. Then he asks them what he can do about it.

Which of these do you do?

A Little Talk about the Bible

1. Is it enough just to read the Bible? What more should you do?
2. Is it enough just to read the Bible and learn what it means? What more should you do?
3. What would you say about Damon, who reads his Bible each day, tries to learn what it means, and tries to do what the Bible says?

Casey, Damon, and Jackie had a little talk. This is what they said.

"I'm glad you read your Bible," Damon said to Casey. "That helps you know what God says."

"I'm glad you ask what it means," Casey said to Jackie. "That helps you know what God wants. From now on I will read my Bible and ask what it means."

"And I'm glad you do what God says in His Word," Jackie said to Damon. "Now when I read my Bible and ask what it means, I will also try to do what it says."

A Little Talk about God and You

1. Why do you want to know *what the Bible says*?
2. Why should you learn *what the Bible means*?
3. Why should you do *what God wants you to do*?

BIBLE READING: James 1:22-25.
BIBLE TRUTH: Don't just read your Bible and learn what it means, but do what it says. From James 1:22.
PRAYER: Dear Lord, let Your Word, the Bible, guide my hands and feet as well as my mind and heart. Amen.

Mother's Singing School

"How do I know that Jesus loves me?" Chelsey asked.

Mother began to sing a little song. It said something like this: "Jesus loves me, this I know, for the Bible tells me so."

Chelsey smiled. "Does Jesus want me to tell others about Him?" she asked.

Mother began to sing another little song. "Jesus wants me for a sunbeam, to shine for Him each day," she sang.

"Do you see how many things you learn about Jesus from little songs?" Mother asked.

Can you think of other little songs that teach you about Jesus?

A Little Talk about Singing

1. Do you know the two songs that Mother sang to Chelsey? Can you sing them?
2. What do you learn about Jesus from these songs? What do you learn about Jesus from other little songs you know?

"Thank you for teaching me about Jesus," said Chelsey. "And thank you for teaching me through these songs. Do other mothers or fathers do this?"

"Many mothers and fathers do this," said Mother. "Mothers and fathers have been doing this for hundreds of years, as long ago as Bible times. The Bible tells us that we should do this."

Then Mother read Colossians 3:16 to Chelsey. Would you like to read it, or have someone read it to you?

A Little Talk about Jesus and You

1. Do you think singing helps us learn something better? Why?
2. Would you like to sing some little songs about Jesus now?

BIBLE READING: Colossians 3:16.
BIBLE TRUTH: Teach and encourage one another by singing psalms, hymns, and godly songs. From Colossians 3:16.
PRAYER: Dear Jesus, I'm so glad I can learn about You by singing. Thank You for being the kind of person I can sing about. Amen.

Is God the Only God?

"Is God the only God?" Doug asked.

"He is the only God who is a real Person," said Mother. "There are many other gods and idols, but they are not real people."

"Then why are they gods if they are not real people?" Doug asked.

A Little Talk about Gods

1. Have you ever wondered if God is the only real God? Are there other gods that people worship?

2. What would you say to Doug? Why are these gods and idols called gods if they are not real people?

"The Bible tells about many gods that Bible-time people worshiped," said Mother. "They were nothing but idols made of wood or stone. They were not real people. But people called them gods. They gave them names."

"I guess having a name makes people think you're a real person," said Doug.

"Yes, but these gods could not listen to their prayers, or make a home in heaven where the people could live forever," said Mother. "They could not help the people when something went wrong."

"I'm glad God is the only real God," said Doug. "I'm glad that He hears me when I pray and that He has a home where I can live with Him forever."

A Little Talk about God and You

1. Why is an idol or other god not really the true God? What can these gods do for you? What can't they do for you? Can they love you? Can they forgive your sins? Can they give you a home in heaven forever?
2. What can God do for you? Are you glad that He is the one true God?

BIBLE READING: Psalm 135:5.
BIBLE TRUTH: God is the only true God. From John 17:3.
PRAYER: Dear God, I'm so glad that You hear my prayers and answer them. I'm glad that You are not made of wood or stone, but are a real live Person who loves me and who made me. Amen.

Recharging Yourself

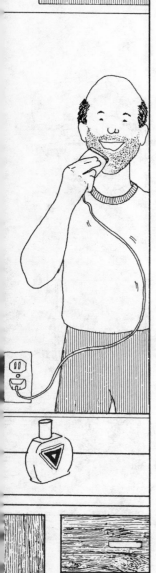

Dirk watched his father turn on his electric razor one morning. But nothing happened. Father laughed. "It works better when I plug it into the electric outlet," he said.

When he did, the razor ran the way it should.

"Electric razors can't do their work without electricity," said Father. "And God's people can't do their work without God."

What do you think Father meant?

A Little Talk about Power

1. Why can't electric razors do their work without electricity? Why can't an electric clock, or toaster, or iron, or stove do its work without electricity?
2. What kind of power do electric things need? What kind of power do God's people need?

"God's people must be plugged into God's power," Father told Dirk.

"How do we do that?" Dirk asked.

"Do you think reading God's Word plugs us into God's power?" Father asked.

Dirk thought about that. He knew that the Bible is God's Word. "I guess we couldn't have much power from God if we didn't know what He says," Dirk said. "We wouldn't know what He wants us to do."

"Do you think praying plugs us into God's power?" Father asked.

Dirk didn't have to think about that very long. "God can't give us much power if we don't even talk to Him," he said.

"Whenever you are like my unplugged razor, read God's Word and pray," said Father. "It will be like plugging you into God, just as I plugged my razor into the electric outlet."

A Little Talk about God and You

1. Why does God have more power than you? How can you get God's power when you need it?
2. Would you like to "plug into" God's power?

BIBLE READING: Isaiah 40:31.
BIBLE TRUTH: Those who trust in the Lord will renew their strength. From Isaiah 40:31.
PRAYER: Dear God, when I need help, remind me to read my Bible and pray. That will help me "plug into" Your power. Thank You for letting me do this. Amen.

Does God Get Tired?

"Does God ever get tired?" Gordon asked.

"Why do you ask?" said Mother.

"Because He does so much work," said Gordon. "He watches over thousands of people. He listens to them pray and takes care of them. And He takes care of the whole world too. Wouldn't you think He would get tired?"

A Little Talk about Getting Tired

1. Do you get tired when you work a long time? What do you do then?
2. Do you think God ever gets tired? What do you think Mother will say to Gordon?

"The Bible tells us that God never gets tired," said Mother. "That's because He does not have a body like ours. We have to eat and sleep to take care of our bodies. That's why we get tired. But since God does not have a body that needs food or sleep, He does not get tired."

A Little Talk about God and You

1. Since God never gets tired, He never needs to sleep. See Psalm 121:4. Do you think He ever stops watching over you?
2. When you and I go to sleep, we stop taking care of our pets. But God never stops taking care of us, does He?
3. Are you glad that God takes care of you all day and all night? Are you glad that He never goes to sleep and forgets about you?

BIBLE READING: Isaiah 40:28-31.

BIBLE TRUTH: God will not grow tired or weary. From Isaiah 40:28.

PRAYER: Thank You, dear God, for watching over me day and night. Thank You for never getting tired so that You do not want to listen to me pray. Amen.

You Wouldn't Steal, Would You?

Keith liked Lee's pen when he saw it lying on his desk at school. There was nothing fancy about it, but it had something special about it. So, when Lee was out of the room, Keith tucked it in his pocket.

Keith pretended that he was studying when Lee came back. But he saw Lee looking for the pen. Lee kept on looking for a long time.

"Did you see anyone take my pen?" Lee asked Keith.

What do you think Keith will say?

A Little Talk about Stealing

1. What is wrong with stealing? Who does it hurt?
2. Do you think Keith will lie so he doesn't get caught stealing? That means he will do something else wrong. What should Keith do?

"No . . . no, I didn't see anyone take your pen," said Keith. But he felt sad and unhappy when he said that. Now he was lying as well as stealing. What would he have to do next?

Keith felt sad all day. That night he was grumpy and quiet at dinner. He found it hard to say his prayers at bedtime. When he prayed, he kept thinking of Lee's pen. He wished he could give it back to Lee and run. But when he prayed, he knew what he would have to do.

The next day Keith gave the pen back to Lee. "I'm really sorry," he said. "I don't know why I took it."

Lee was so happy to have his pen back. "It's a special pen to me," Lee said. "It wouldn't be worth much to you, but my grandfather gave it to me the day before he died."

Now you know why Keith was very happy that he gave Lee's pen back to him.

A Little Talk about God and You

1. Why does God not want us to steal? Do you think stealing hurts Him? Why would He be hurt more when God's friends steal something?
2. How would you feel if a good friend stole something from you? What would you say to this friend if you found that he had taken something from you?

BIBLE READING: Exodus 20:15.
BIBLE TRUTH: You must not steal. From Exodus 20:15.
PRAYER: Dear God, if I am ever tempted to steal, remind me quickly of what You have said. Amen.

Wise Friends and Foolish Friends

One boy chose bad friends. They often lied, cheated, and stole things. They said dirty words and talked about dirty things. Before long this boy lied, cheated, stole things, and said dirty words.

A second boy chose good friends. They told the truth, were fair, and respected the belongings of others. They spoke nicely to each other. When they had to make a choice, they asked God and wise people to help them.

The second boy told the truth, was fair, and respected the property of others. He said fun and caring words.

A Little Talk about Wise and Foolish Friends

1. What happened to the first boy after he was around his foolish friends for a while? Why do you think this happened?
2. What happened to the second boy after he was around his wise friends for a while? Why do you think this happened?

Do you suppose we become like our friends and our friends become like us?

A Little Talk about Jesus and You

1. What kind of friend does Jesus want to be? Is He a wise Friend or a foolish friend?
2. What kind of friend do you want to be to Jesus? Will you be a wise friend to Him?
3. What kind of friends do you want to choose? Why? What kind of friend do you want to be to other people? Why?

BIBLE READING: 1 Corinthians 15:33.
BIBLE TRUTH: A person who has wise friends grows wiser, but a person who has foolish friends grows more foolish. From Proverbs 13:20.
PRAYER: Dear Jesus, teach me to choose the right friends who are wise and not foolish. Most of all, be my best Friend and show me the way I should live. Amen.

Consider Your Ways

A boy had a bad habit. He often lied about things. So people did not believe him even when he told the truth.

A girl had a problem. She often cheated at school. Her friends knew that she did this, so they did not trust her even when she did not cheat.

A man had a problem. He stole money from his company. The other people at the company knew this, so they did not trust him.

A woman had a bad habit. She gossiped and said bad things about others. She even said bad things about her friends. Of course she did not have many friends.

What would you like to say to these four people?

A Little Talk about Your Ways

1. Do you ever lie, cheat, steal, or gossip? If you do, your friends know about it. You can't hide things like that.

2. What did you want to say to these four people? Do you want to say any of these things to yourself?

The psalmwriter once thought about the things that he did wrong. He knew he was not pleasing God. So he said, "I have considered my ways, and have turned my steps to God's Word" (from Psalm 119:59).

To the boy who lied, would you say, "Consider your ways"?

To the girl who cheated, would you say, "Consider your ways"?

To the man who stole, would you say, "Consider your ways"?

To the woman who gossiped, would you say, "Consider your ways"?

"Consider your ways" is another way of saying, "Think about what you are doing." Then with the psalmwriter you can say, "I have turned my steps to God's Word."

A Little Talk about God and You

1. Why should each of these people consider his or her ways? What should they do then?
2. Is this a good time to consider your ways? After you do, what should you do then?

BIBLE READING: Psalm 119:59.

BIBLE TRUTH: I have considered my ways and have turned to God's Word. From Psalm 119:59.

PRAYER: Dear God, I want to think about my ways. Guide my steps to where they should go according to Your Word, the Bible. Amen.

Think about what you are doing

Why You Should Not Do Some Things

"I would not do that," a boy told his friends one day.

"Why not?" they asked.

"Because my father would not do it," he answered.

"I would not do that," a girl told her friends one day.

"Why not?" they asked.

"Because my mother would not do it," she answered.

Can you think of another good reason not to do something wrong?

A Little Talk about Right and Wrong

1. Why would the boy not do something wrong?
2. Why would the girl not do something wrong?
3. Think of some things your friends might want you to do, but your mother or father would not do.

"I would not do that," a girl told her friends one day.

"Why not?" they asked.

"Because Jesus would not do it," she answered.

If Jesus would not do it, should you?

A Little Talk about Jesus and You

1. What does it mean for a person to set a good example? How do your parents set a good example for you?
2. How does Jesus set a good example for you? What are some things your friends might want you to do that Jesus would not do? Why should you not do them? Do you set a good example for other people?

BIBLE READING: 1 Peter 2:21.
BIBLE TRUTH: Follow my example, as I follow the example of Christ. From 1 Corinthians 11:1.
PRAYER: Dear Jesus, thank You for doing what is good and not doing what is bad. Help me to do what You would do. Amen.

The Meanest Kid in School

"He's the meanest kid in school," said Stan.

Father smiled. "Perhaps someone needs to do something kind for him," he said.

Stan thought about that when he went to school. He thought about it when he saw the meanest kid in school. Someone should do something kind for him. But Stan didn't want to do it.

Then Stan saw that the meanest kid in school had forgotten to bring a pencil. Stan had two pencils. What should he do?

A Little Talk about Sharing

1. What would you like to say to Stan now? What would you do if you were Stan?
2. Do you know someone in school who is mean or grouchy? What do you think would happen if someone did something kind to this person?

"I have an extra pencil," Stan said to the meanest kid in school. "Would you like to use it today?"

The meanest kid didn't seem mean anymore. "Thanks," he said. And he even smiled.

A Little Talk about Jesus and You

1. Why do you think Jesus was pleased with what Stan did?
2. What would you do if someone continued to be mean even after you were kind?

BIBLE READING: Luke 6:27-36.
BIBLE TRUTH: Do good to your enemies. Lend to them even when you don't expect to get anything back. Luke 6:35.
PRAYER: Thank You, Jesus, for telling us how to treat our enemies. You know I would try to hurt my enemy instead of help him, and that is not Your way of doing things. Amen.

Be Patient

"Why can't you learn to color within the lines?" an older brother grumbled.

"Why can't I have a new bike?" a girl complained.

"Why do I have to wait until I'm older to go downtown by myself?" a little boy argued.

What do you think someone should say to these boys and girls about being patient?

A Little Talk about Being Patient

1. What is the problem with each boy or girl above? Would you say each of these is patient or impatient? Why?
2. When was the last time you were impatient about something? What was it? Why did you not want to wait?

Why do you think the little girl did not color within the lines? Was she old enough? Was she ready to do this even if her older brother showed her how?

Why do you think the girl did not have her new bike? Would grumbling or complaining get it for her?

Why do you think the little boy could not go downtown by himself? Why should he wait until he is older?

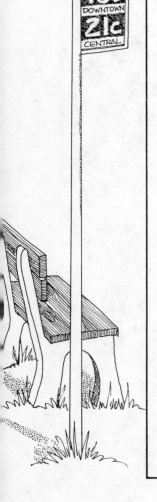

Why do you have to wait for some things? Why don't you get everything you want, *right now*?

A Little Talk about God and You

1. Is God in a hurry? Do you think God wants to do everything today? Will He wait to do some special things tomorrow and the day after tomorrow?

2. Is God pleased when we want everything to happen right now? Why not? Why does God want us to learn to wait? Why does He want us to learn to be patient with other people?

BIBLE READING: James 1:4.
BIBLE TRUTH: Be patient toward others. From 1 Thessalonians 5:14.
PRAYER: Dear God, You are not in a hurry. Teach me to be patient, as You are patient. Amen.

Ugly Places

"Yuk, what an ugly place!" Andrea said to Mother.

Andrea's mother was getting her car fixed at a little garage. On the other side of the street garbage trucks roared in and out of a dump. It was noisy and dusty, and the place smelled. Andrea was afraid to move. She thought she would get grease or dirt on her pretty pink dress.

"It's not beautiful like the mountains and lakes we saw on our vacation," Mother said. "But what would you say if I told you this is a holy place?"

Andrea looked surprised. Wouldn't you?

A Little Talk about Holy Places

1. Think about some ugly places you have seen. Did you think they were holy? Why not?
2. Why would Mother say this ugly place was holy? What do you think she will say to Andrea?

"How could this be a holy place?" asked Andrea. "There is no church here, and it's so terribly ugly."

"Many years ago a man named Moses was far away from home," said Mother. "He was in a desert. There were not many beautiful things there—just sand and mountains. But God told Moses this was a holy place. Do you know why?"

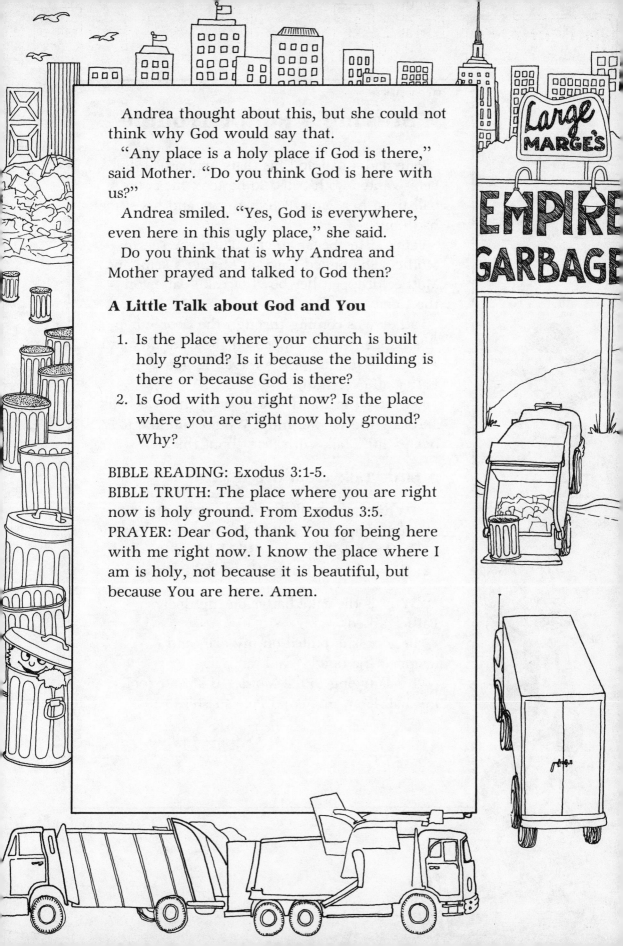

Andrea thought about this, but she could not think why God would say that.

"Any place is a holy place if God is there," said Mother. "Do you think God is here with us?"

Andrea smiled. "Yes, God is everywhere, even here in this ugly place," she said.

Do you think that is why Andrea and Mother prayed and talked to God then?

A Little Talk about God and You

1. Is the place where your church is built holy ground? Is it because the building is there or because God is there?
2. Is God with you right now? Is the place where you are right now holy ground? Why?

BIBLE READING: Exodus 3:1-5.
BIBLE TRUTH: The place where you are right now is holy ground. From Exodus 3:5.
PRAYER: Dear God, thank You for being here with me right now. I know the place where I am is holy, not because it is beautiful, but because You are here. Amen.

Stirring a Pot of Trouble

Pete had a ball and his sister had a ball. But Pete wanted both balls. So he took his sister's ball from her. Now Pete had two and his sister had none.

Pete's sister began to cry. Then she ran to Mother. She pulled hard on Mother's arm, and Mother dropped her bowl of cake batter on the floor.

Father was coming through the door when this happened. He slipped on the cake mix and fell in the middle of the mess. He got cake batter all over him.

Pete stood in the doorway with the two balls and saw the whole thing. Would you like to have a little talk with Pete about this?

A Little Talk about Greed

1. What started all this trouble? Would it have happened if Pete had not been greedy and wanted his sister's ball?
2. What do you think Pete should say now?

"Why is the cake batter on the floor?" Father asked.

"Because she pulled on my arm and I dropped the bowl," said Mother.

"I was trying to tell Mother that Pete took my ball from me," said Pete's sister.

"I...I'm sorry," said Pete. "I really caused a lot of trouble."

So Pete's sister forgave him for taking the ball. And Mother forgave Pete's sister for pulling on her arm. And after Pete cleaned up the cake batter mess, the whole family went out to play ball.

A Little Talk about Jesus and You

1. What did you learn about greed? What did you learn about forgiveness?
2. Are you ever greedy and want something that someone else has? Remember the pot of trouble that Pete brought to his family.

BIBLE READING: Proverbs 15:27.
BIBLE TRUTH: A greedy person brings trouble to his family. From Proverbs 15:27.
PRAYER: Dear Jesus, teach me to share and not be greedy. And teach me to forgive when a greedy friend brings me trouble. Amen.

Are You God's Son or Daughter?

Dave had been reading a story about a ship in Jesus' time. Slaves rowed this ship. They worked very hard. The man in charge whipped them to make them work harder.

"I'm glad I'm not a slave," said Dave. "That was terrible."

"Do you like being a son better?" Father asked.

Dave smiled. "Much better," he said.

"Aren't you glad God calls you His son instead of His slave?" Father asked.

A Little Talk about Being a Son or Daughter

1. How would you like to be a slave? Why not? Are you glad you are a son or daughter instead? Why?
2. What are some of the good things you get because you are a son or daughter?

"What are some of the good things you get because you are my son?" Father asked.

Dave thought a little while. Then he gave a long list of things. "You help me have good food to eat and clothes to wear," he said. "You love me and take good care of me. You comfort me when I'm hurt. You listen to me when I need to tell someone my troubles."

"What good things do we get because we are God's son or daughter?" Father asked.

Dave thought about this. He had a long list, but these things seemed so much like Father's list. "God helps us have good food to eat and clothes to wear," he said. "He loves us and takes good care of us. He comforts us when we're hurt. He listens to us when we need to tell someone our troubles."

"That's why God is like a father or mother," said Father. "Or should I say that's why fathers and mothers should be like God."

"I'm glad I'm your son and God's son!" said Dave. "But I want to do good things for you. And I want to do good things for God, too."

A Little Talk about God and You

1. What are some of the good things that God does for you? Are these the kinds of things a good father or mother does for a child?
2. What are some of the good things you do for God? Are these the kinds of things a good son or daughter does for parents?

BIBLE READING: 2 Corinthians 6:18.
BIBLE TRUTH: I will be a Father to you, and you will be My sons and daughters. From 2 Corinthians 6:18.
PRAYER: Dear God, thank You for being a Father. That's a wonderful idea. Thank You for letting me be Your son or daughter. Amen.

Why Was I Crying?

"Why was I crying last night?" Faye asked Mother.

"You pinched your finger in the door," said Mother. "Does it feel all right now?"

Faye touched her finger. "It's still a little sore," she said. "But it's not sore enough to make me cry."

"Well, you certainly look like a sunbeam this morning," said Mother. "Tears last night, sunshine this morning. That's the way God said it would be."

"He did?" Faye asked. "When did God say that?"

A Little Talk about Tears

1. Have you ever cried about something at night, then woke up to find everything better?
2. Do you know where God said something about tears at night and sunshine in the morning?

"It's found in Psalm 30:5," said Mother. "This is talking about times when God has to teach us things that can make us cry. But it's true about other times, too."

Then Mother read Psalm 30:5 to Faye. Would you like to read it too?

A Little Talk about God and You

1. When you have to cry about something, who do you want to comfort you? Mother? Father? God? Why?
2. When Mother or Father hurt about something, do you try to comfort them? Do you try to turn their sad time into sunshine? Do you pray and ask God to do that too?

BIBLE READING: Psalm 30:5.

BIBLE TRUTH: You may cry all night, but in the morning the sun will rise and things will seem all right again. From Psalm 30:5.

PRAYER: Dear God, thank You for the morning sun that takes away the night, and takes away my tears. Amen.

If You Can't Sing, What Can You Do?

"I need four people for the program," said the Sunday school teacher. "First I need someone who can sing well."

One girl held up her hand. "I can sing," she said.

"Yes, you sing very well," said the teacher. "Now I need someone who plays the piano."

A boy held up his hand. "I can do that," he said.

The teacher smiled. She knew the boy could play well. Another boy said he could read the Bible and another girl said she would pray.

"Good," said the teacher. "Each of you can do something well. That's like hands and feet, eyes and nose working together."

A Little Talk about Talents

1. What can you do well? Can you play baseball well? Can you sing well or play a musical instrument well? What else can you do?
2. Can you do something well that a friend cannot do well? Can a friend do something well that you cannot do well?
3. Remember the four friends above? Each can do one thing well. Now think how much fun they will have doing what they can do together!

"How would you like to have four noses but no eyes?" the teacher asked. "Or how would you like four hands but no feet? Think of the things you could not do. But think of the special things you *can* do because you have eyes, ears, hands, feet, mouth, and other things that work together."

That does seem much better than having four eyes but no nose, or four feet but no hands, doesn't it?

A Little Talk about God and You

1. Why do you think God gave you hands, feet, ears, eyes, and mouth? Why didn't He give you four of one and none of the other? How would you like that?
2. If you are glad that God made you the way He did, why not thank Him now?
3. If you are glad that God gave you a special talent, why not thank Him now for that? Then use your special talent to help God do His work.

BIBLE READING: Romans 12:4-8.
BIBLE TRUTH: We have different gifts that God has given us. Use them cheerfully! From Romans 12:6-8.
PRAYER: Thank You, dear God, for giving me eyes, ears, hands, feet, and mouth in just the right way. Help me do what I can do best, and do it for You. Amen.

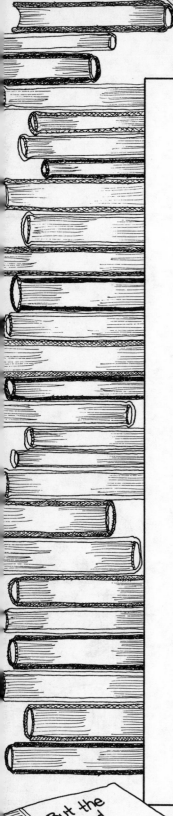

How Long Does the Bible Last?

"My Bible is almost falling apart," said Marcy. "I don't think it will last very much longer."

Father looked at Marcy's Bible. It really was falling apart.

"It's time to get you a new one," said Father. This time we will get you one that is made a little better."

"If my Bible falls apart, does that hurt the Bible itself?" asked Marcy.

A Little Talk about the Bible

1. Have you ever had a copy of the Bible that fell apart? Did you get a new one?
2. If one copy of the Bible falls apart, does it mean that God's Word, the Bible, has fallen apart? Why not? There are thousands of other copies, aren't there?

"The Bible is God's Word," said Father. "All the words are God's words. People print these words, or write them, in books or on napkins or on all kinds of things. Your Bible is a printed book. People print millions of copies. We lose some copies, some are thrown away, and some fall apart, like yours. We could lose a million copies of the Bible, but we will never lose the Bible itself. God's Word will always be here for us to read."

But the Word of the Lord abides forever
1 Peter 1:25

"What if every Bible on earth was lost?" Marcy asked.

"That won't happen," said Father. "There are too many copies. But even if it did, God has His Word written in heaven. It will never go away. It will always be there, even if the whole earth is destroyed."

"I'm glad I can have a copy of God's Word," said Marcy. "I'm especially glad that you will get me a new copy."

A Little Talk about God and You

1. How long will God's Word be with us? If you lose your copy of the Bible, does that mean the Bible is lost? Why not?
2. Can anyone do anything to take God's Word away completely? Why not?

BIBLE READING: Psalm 119:89.
BIBLE TRUTH: Your Word, O Lord, is forever. It is there in heaven, and will never be taken away. From Psalm 119:89.
PRAYER: Thank You, dear God, that Your Word can never be taken away from us. Amen.

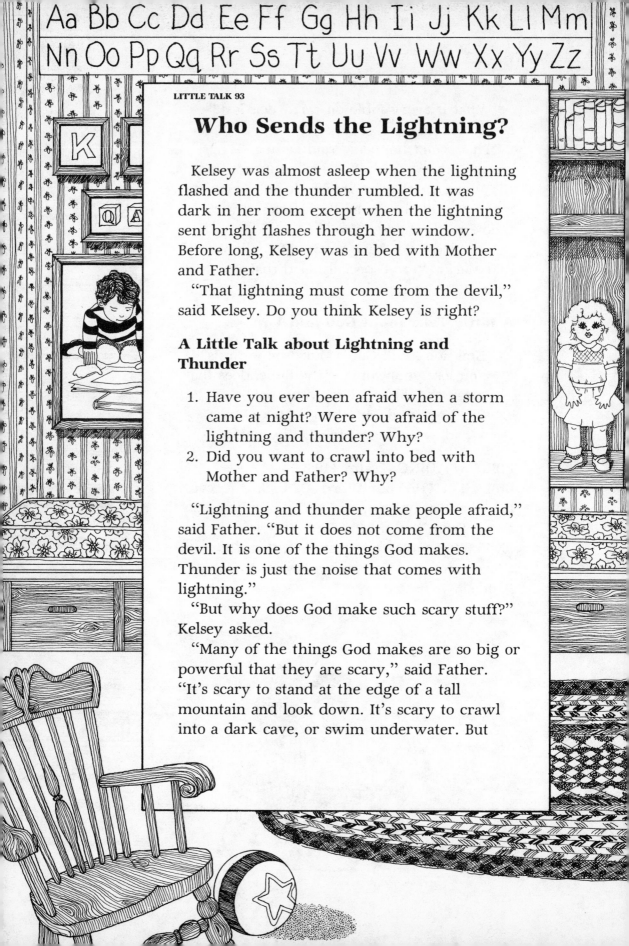

Who Sends the Lightning?

Kelsey was almost asleep when the lightning flashed and the thunder rumbled. It was dark in her room except when the lightning sent bright flashes through her window. Before long, Kelsey was in bed with Mother and Father.

"That lightning must come from the devil," said Kelsey. Do you think Kelsey is right?

A Little Talk about Lightning and Thunder

1. Have you ever been afraid when a storm came at night? Were you afraid of the lightning and thunder? Why?
2. Did you want to crawl into bed with Mother and Father? Why?

"Lightning and thunder make people afraid," said Father. "But it does not come from the devil. It is one of the things God makes. Thunder is just the noise that comes with lightning."

"But why does God make such scary stuff?" Kelsey asked.

"Many of the things God makes are so big or powerful that they are scary," said Father. "It's scary to stand at the edge of a tall mountain and look down. It's scary to crawl into a dark cave, or swim underwater. But

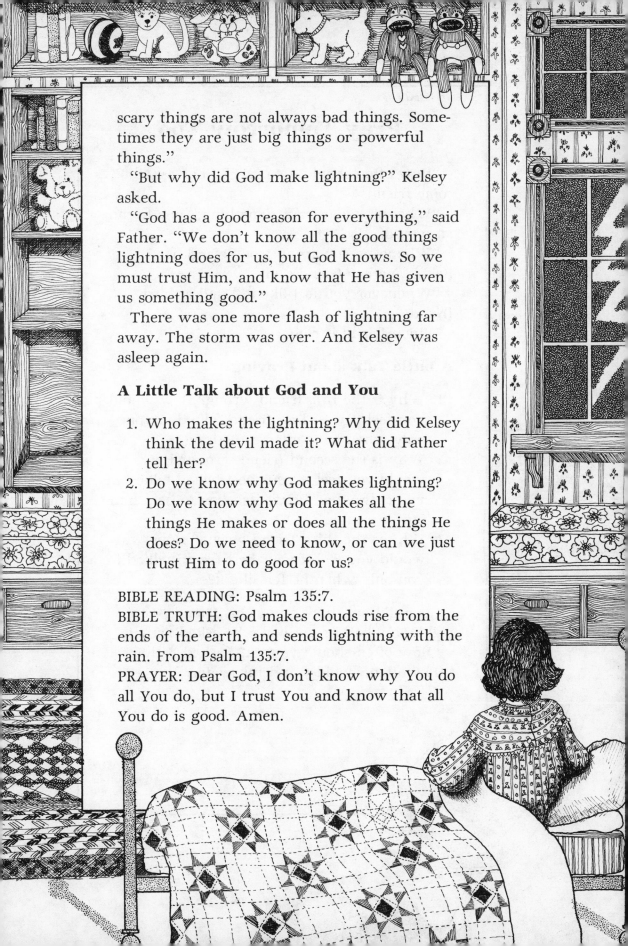

scary things are not always bad things. Sometimes they are just big things or powerful
things."

"But why did God make lightning?" Kelsey
asked.

"God has a good reason for everything," said
Father. "We don't know all the good things
lightning does for us, but God knows. So we
must trust Him, and know that He has given
us something good."

There was one more flash of lightning far
away. The storm was over. And Kelsey was
asleep again.

A Little Talk about God and You

1. Who makes the lightning? Why did Kelsey
   think the devil made it? What did Father
   tell her?
2. Do we know why God makes lightning?
   Do we know why God makes all the
   things He makes or does all the things He
   does? Do we need to know, or can we just
   trust Him to do good for us?

BIBLE READING: Psalm 135:7.
BIBLE TRUTH: God makes clouds rise from the
ends of the earth, and sends lightning with the
rain. From Psalm 135:7.
PRAYER: Dear God, I don't know why You do
all You do, but I trust You and know that all
You do is good. Amen.

Pray Tomorrow Too

"How often should we pray?" Gene asked some friends.

"Whenever you want something," one friend answered.

"Whenever you are in trouble and need help," another friend said.

"Whenever you feel like it," said a third friend.

Which friend is right?

A Little Talk about Praying

1. Why is the first friend wrong? How would you feel if your best friend talked to you only when he wanted something?
2. Why is the second friend wrong? How would you feel if your best friend talked to you only when he wanted you to help him out of trouble?
3. Why is the third friend wrong? How would you feel if your best friend talked to you only when he felt like it?

Gene did not think any of his friends were right. So when he got home he asked Father.

"How often should you eat?" asked Father. "How often should you drink water?"

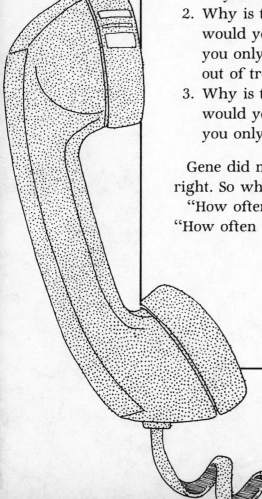

Gene smiled. "Several times each day," he said.

"Should we pray less than we eat or drink?" asked Father. "Do we need God any less than we need food and water?"

Do you think Father is right?

A Little Talk about God and You

1. How often do you eat and drink water during each day? How often do you pray?
2. How often do you think God wants you to talk with Him? Will you remember to pray tomorrow too?

BIBLE READING: Romans 12:12.
BIBLE TRUTH: Be faithful in prayer. From Romans 12:12.
PRAYER: Dear God, I want to talk to You often. Help me to remember to do that. Amen.

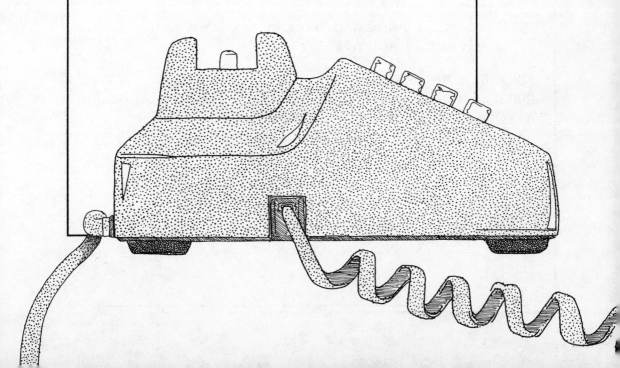

Wait!

"When may I open my birthday presents?" Harold whispered to Mother.

"Shhh," said Mother. "You know that you must wait until the end of the birthday party."

"But I can't wait!" said Harold. "I want to open them now."

A Little Talk about Waiting

1. Do you think Harold is patient or impatient?
2. Why should Harold wait to open his gifts? Why not open them now?
3. Harold said, "I can't wait." Do you think that is true? What would you like to say to Harold?

"What would Jesus tell you if He were here?" Mother asked.

Harold thought about that. "I think He would tell me to wait," he said.

Do you think Harold is right? Would Jesus tell him to wait?

A Little Talk about Jesus and You

1. What would Jesus say if you said, "I want You to answer my prayer *now*"?
2. What would Jesus say if you said, "I can't wait to get a new bike; I want it *today*"?

BIBLE READING: Isaiah 30:18.

BIBLE TRUTH: You will be blessed if you wait for the Lord to do what He wants. From Isaiah 30:18.

PRAYER: Dear Jesus, teach me to wait when I want to run faster than You want me to run. Amen.

Doing Something about Your Hopes

Once there were two boys. Each boy's father had lost his job. The boys were talking about this.

"I hope my father gets a job soon," said Del. "But I'm worried because I don't think he will. Then we won't have enough money to take care of us."

"I hope my father gets a job soon, too," said Mel. "I have been praying every day about this. I'm excited because I think God will give him just the right job."

A Little Talk about Hope

1. What was Mel doing that Del was not doing? Why should this make a difference?
2. Why do you think Mel is excited and Del is not?
3. Is it enough to just hope for something? What else should we do?

Mel's mother heard what the two boys said. "I have a Bible verse for you," she said. "Be joyful in hope and faithful in prayer. That is from Romans 12:12."

"What does it mean?" asked Del.

"Do you want something very much?" asked Mel's mother.

"Yes, I want my father to get the right job," said Del.

"This Bible verse says that you should do more than just hope for it," said Mel's mother. "You must hope and pray. When you ask God to help, your hope will be joyful, or exciting."

"Is that why Mel is excited about his father's job?" Del asked.

"I'm sure it is," said Mel's mother.

"Then I'm going to pray every day for my father to get the right job," said Del. "I want to hope joyfully too!"

A Little Talk about God and You

1. What did Del and Mel hope would happen? What are some things you hope will happen?
2. Why is it not enough just to hope that something will happen? Why is it important to ask God to help you?
3. How does being "faithful in prayer" help you to be "joyful in hope"?

BIBLE READING: Romans 12:12.
BIBLE TRUTH: Being faithful in prayer will help you to be joyful in hope. From Romans 12:12.
PRAYER: Dear God, help me to remember to pray much about the things I hope for. Then I will be joyful as I expect You to answer. Amen.

WESTSIDE
PRECINCT 5

A Special Kind of Flag

"Look at that flag!" said Herb. "It's the biggest flag I've ever seen."

"What kind of flag is that?" Uncle Dan asked.

"It's the flag of our country," said Herb.

"That's right," said Uncle Dan. "Wherever you see that flag, you think of our country. Do you remember another kind of flag in the front of our church?"

"There's a white one with some stuff on it," said Herb.

"That's the Christian flag," said Uncle Dan. "Wherever you see that, you think of Christians. There are many different kinds of flags. Each kind reminds us of a different country, or state, or something else. Did you know that God has a special flag over you?"

A Little Talk about Flags

1. What kind of flag did Herb see? What can you tell about the flag of your country? Can you tell all the different things that are on it? What does each thing mean?
2. Have you seen the white Christian flag? What are some things on it?
3. Uncle Dan told Herb about God's flag. What do you think that is?

"The Bible tells us about this flag," said Uncle Dan. "Let me read it to you."

Uncle Dan read from the Song of Solomon 2:4: "His banner over me is love."

"A banner is a flag," said Uncle Dan. "This tells us that God has some kind of flag over His people. Our country's flag over a building says that the building is part of our country. God's flag over us says that we belong to Him."

"I'm glad God has put His flag over me," said Herb. "I'm glad He loves me enough to say that I belong to Him."

A Little Talk about God and You

1. Are you glad that God has His flag of love over you? Are you glad that He loves you enough to say that you belong to Him?
2. Would you be willing for others to see God's flag over you? Would you be willing to tell your friends that you belong to Him?

BIBLE READING: Song of Solomon 2:1,4.
BIBLE TRUTH: His flag over me is love. From Song of Solomon 2:4.
PRAYER: Dear God, thank You for putting Your flag of love over me. I know that You are not ashamed to love me. I should never be ashamed of You either. Amen.

Pride

There was once a very tall man. He was a foot taller than all the other little people who lived in his village. This man was almost five feet tall!

Since this five-foot-tall man was taller than all his friends, he was very proud. Other people in his village looked up to him and said good things about him but this man looked down on them and said bad things about them.

A Little Talk about Pride

1. Do you think this five-foot-tall man was proud? How do you know? Why should he not be proud?
2. What is wrong with being proud because you are taller or smarter or richer than other people? What would you say to a person like this?

One day a stranger came to the village. He was a tall stranger, more than six feet tall. The five-foot-tall man suddenly had to look up to another person.

This man had never known that there were people taller than he. He had always thought he was the tallest person in the world.

This five-foot-tall man did not want the taller man to think he was better because he was taller. So from that time on, he could never think he was better than his shorter friends.

A Little Talk about Jesus and You

1. Have you seen people who think they are better than others because they are taller or smarter or richer? They need to meet Jesus, don't they? They can never think they are more important than He is.
2. Why should Jesus' friends never think they are more important than other people?

BIBLE READING: Romans 12:3.
BIBLE TRUTH: Do not think of yourself more highly than you ought to think. From Romans 12:3.
PRAYER: Dear Jesus, help me never to be proud or to think I am better than others. If I ever do, help me to think about You. Amen.

Why Do I Sleep?

"I don't want to go to bed," Liz grumbled. "I want to stay up all night and play. I don't want to waste time sleeping anymore. There are too many fun things to do."

Mother and Father looked at each other. "All right," said Father. "You do not have to sleep anymore. Tomorrow we will sell your bed and give the money to some poor family."

Mother and Father went to the living room to read. Liz looked at her bed. What do you think she is thinking now?

A Little Talk about Sleep

1. Have you ever said what Liz said? Have you ever thought you would like to stay up all night, or stop sleeping so you could play more?
2. What do you think will happen to Liz?

Liz did not like what Father said about selling her bed. She did not want him to do that. But of course she would not need it anymore if she wasn't going to sleep.

Liz played with her dolls. Then she colored in a coloring book. She began to yawn. She played with a game she got for her birthday. Now she yawned several times.

Later, when Mother and Father were ready for bed, they looked into Liz's room. There was Liz, lying on her bed, sleeping soundly.

"God gives sleep to those He loves," Father said to Liz the next morning.

Liz smiled. "I guess God loves me," she said.

A Little Talk about God and You

1. Why does God give you sleep? What would happen to your body if you never slept? What does sleep do for you?
2. Does sleep tell us that God loves us? How do you know?

BIBLE READING: Psalm 127:2.
BIBLE TRUTH: God gives sleep to those He loves. From Psalm 127:2.
PRAYER: Dear God, thank You for the gift of sleep. I know this is one way You show that You love me. Amen.

When Do You Obey?

"Eddie, you know Mother doesn't want you to put your feet on the sofa!" Eddie's little sister shouted.

"But Mother isn't here now!" said Eddie.

A Little Talk about Obeying

1. When should you obey—only when Mother or Father are with you?
2. Why should you obey Mother and Father when they are not with you?

"Then you should pretend Mother is here!" said Eddie's little sister.

Eddie thought about that. He knew what Mother would say if she were in the living room with him. He knew that Mother would not like what he was doing.

"Okay, okay!" said Eddie. Then he took his feet off the sofa.

Eddie really did want to obey Mother, whether she was there with him or far away.

A Little Talk about Jesus and You

1. Do you want to please Jesus? Do you want to please Him only at certain times, or do you want to please Him and obey Him at all times?
2. Sometimes Jesus seems far away. Then we are tempted to do things that do not please Him. But Jesus is always with us, isn't He? When He seems far away, pretend that He is there with you, looking at you. That's the way it is, because Jesus really is there, looking at you.

BIBLE READING: Ephesians 6:1-4.

BIBLE TRUTH: Children, obey your parents in the Lord, for this is right. From Ephesians 6:1.

PRAYER: Dear Jesus, help me to remember to obey You and my parents at all times, and not just some of the time. Amen.

Topical and Biblical Guide

TOPICAL GUIDE

ADVICE: A wise person listens to good advice.   Little Talk 15
Proverbs 12:15

AGE: Let's be happy with our age, since we can't change it.   Little Talk 14
Proverbs 20:29

ANGER: Sin makes God angry.   Little Talk 24
Romans 1:18-20

ANGER: Don't stay angry after sunset.   Little Talk 28
Ephesians 4:26,27

ARGUING: Don't argue! Live at peace with others.   Little Talk 23
Romans 12:18

ASHAMED: If you are ashamed of Jesus, He will be ashamed   Little Talk 29
of you. Luke 12:8,9

BAD WAYS: We should turn from bad ways to God's Word.   Little Talk 83
Psalm 119:59

BEAUTY: Everything God has made is beautiful.   Little Talks 20,13
Ecclesiastes 3:11

BIBLE: God's Word lasts forever.   Little Talk 92
Psalm 119:89

BIBLE: God's Word is sweeter than honey or candy.   Little Talk 67
Psalm 119:102-104

BIBLE: Read your Bible, learn what it means, and do what it says. Little Talk 76
James 1:22-25

BRAGGING: Don't brag. Let others praise you.   Little Talk 50
Psalm 27:1,2

CAN'T: Is it really something you can't do, or won't do?   Little Talk 74
Matthew 19:26

CHRISTIAN LIFE: Our lives for Jesus are like a bright path.   Little Talk 37
Proverbs 4:18,19

COMFORT: God will comfort us.   Little Talk 90
Psalm 30:5

HONESTY: When we don't give what we should, we rob God. Malachi 3:8-12

HONESTY: God does not want us to accept bribes. Deuteronomy 16:19; Mark 14:10,11

HONESTY: God sees everything we do. Proverbs 5:21,22

HURTFUL WORDS: They come from the heart through the mouth. Matthew 15:17-20

JESUS: You must be for Jesus or against Him. Matthew 12:30

JUDGING OTHERS: We must not judge others by how they look. 1 Samuel 16:7

LOVE: God's love will never fail us. Psalm 119:76

LOVE: God tells the whole world that He loves us. Song of Solomon 2:1,4

LOVE: Show love by what you say and do. John 3:16; 1 John 3:18

LYING: Lying makes us sad, so tell the truth. John 14:6; Philippians 4:8,9

MONEY: Don't love money too much. Matthew 6:21; 1 Timothy 6:10

OBEYING: Obey your parents, and obey at all times. Ephesians 6:1-4

OLDER PEOPLE: Be polite when you talk to them. 1 Timothy 5:1

PARENTS: God is like a father or mother to me. 2 Corinthians 6:18

PATIENCE: We must learn to wait patiently for the Lord. Isaiah 30:18

PATIENCE: Be as patient with others as you want God to be with you. 1 Corinthians 13:4

PATIENCE: Learn to be patient, as God is patient. 1 Thessalonians 5:14; James 1:4

PRAYER: When does God answer prayer? Psalm 37:5-7

PRAYER: When you pray, God is near, listening to you. Psalm 145:17-19

PRAYER: God's people need to talk with Him often.   Little Talks 94,96
Romans 12:12

PRIDE: Don't be proud of yourself or brag about yourself.   Little Talk 98
Romans 12:3

QUARRELING: Don't quarrel, especially with yourself.   Little Talk 47
Matthew 12:25-28

QUIETNESS: We will learn more about God when we are quiet.   Little Talk 56
Psalm 46:7-11

SAFETY: God is like a fortress, for He keeps us safe.   Little Talk 3
2 Samuel 22:2; Jeremiah 16:19

SALVATION: It is like a beautiful piece of clothing.   Little Talk 64
Isaiah 61:10

SEASONS: God gives good things with each season.   Little Talk 20
Genesis 1:14

SERVING: Serve God with the gifts He gives.   Little Talk 19
Deuteronomy 8:17,18

SIN: Only Jesus can wash away our sin.   Little Talk 7
Matthew 9:6; 1 John 1:7

SINGING: We should sing praises to the Lord.   Little Talk 65
Exodus 15:1,2; Psalm 47:6

SINGING: The earth sings to the Lord, like a great choir.   Little Talk 17
Psalm 96:1; Psalm 96:11-13

SINGING: We should teach and help one another by singing.   Little Talk 77
Colossians 3:16

SLEEP: Sleep is God's gift to those He loves.   Little Talk 99
Psalm 127:2

STARS: God has given each star a name.   Little Talk 25
Isaiah 40:25,26

STEALING: God commands us not to steal.   Little Talk 81
Exodus 20:15

STRENGTH: We grow stronger when we are happy in the Lord.   Little Talk 12
Nehemiah 8:10; Psalm 27:1

STRENGTH: We get new strength from the Lord.   Little Talk 79
Isaiah 40:31

SWEARING: If you swear, someday you will have to tell God why.   Little Talk 32
Matthew 12:35-37

SYMPATHY: We should laugh and cry with others.   Little Talk 61
Romans 12:15

TALENTS: God has given each of us different talents.   Little Talk 91
Romans 12:4-8

TRUST: God is the Person we can trust completely.
Psalm 37:3

TRUTH: Say what you really mean, or you are lying.
Romans 12:9

UGLY PLACES: Every place is holy because God is there.
Exodus 3:1-5

WANTING GOD: We get thirsty for God as we do for water.
Psalm 42:1,2; John 4:14

WORK: We should finish the work we begin.
Joshua 11:15

WORK: Our fingers and hands should do God's work.
Psalm 90:16,17

WORRY: Worry is like weeds, choking out God's Word.
Mark 4:13-20

WORSHIP: God is the only true God.
Psalm 135:5

BIBLICAL GUIDE

2 Corinthians 9:6-8
GIVING: Give cheerfully, even if it isn't much.

Little Talk 4

Galatians 5:13-15
HELPING: Help God and His friends do His work.

Little Talk 46

Ephesians 4:26,27
ANGER: Don't stay angry after sunset.

Little Talk 28

Ephesians 6:1-4
OBEYING: Obey your parents, and obey at all times.

Little Talks 33,
100

Philippians 4:8,9
LYING: Tell the truth about one another. You will feel better.

Little Talk 69

Colossians 3:16
SINGING: We should teach and help one another by singing.

Little Talk 77

1 Thessalonians 5:14
PATIENCE: Learn to be patient, as God is patient.

Little Talk 86

1 Timothy 5:1
OLDER PEOPLE: Be polite when you talk to them.

Little Talk 30

1 Timothy 6:10
MONEY: Never love money more than God.

Little Talk 68

James 1:4
PATIENCE: Learn to be patient, as God is patient.

Little Talk 86

James 1:17
GIFTS: Every good and perfect gift comes from God.

Little Talk 63

James 1:22-25
BIBLE: Read your Bible, learn what it means, and do what it says.

Little Talk 76

1 Peter 2:21
EXAMPLE: Follow the example of those who follow Jesus.

Little Talk 84

1 Peter 5:8,9
DEVIL: The devil is like a roaring lion who wants to hurt you.

Little Talk 42

1 John 1:7
SIN: Jesus alone can wash away our sins.

Little Talk 7

1 John 3:18
LOVE: Show love by what you say and do.

Little Talk 36